Translating Love

Translating Love

Michael Wogsland

Elm Hill
A Division of
HarperCollins Christian Publishing

www.elmhillbooks.com

© 2018 Michael Wogsland

Translating Love

All rights reserved. No portion of this book may be reproduced, stored in a retrieval system, or transmitted in any form or by any means—electronic, mechanical, photocopy, recording, scanning, or other—except for brief quotations in critical reviews or articles, without the prior written permission of the publisher.

Published in Nashville, Tennessee, by Elm Hill, an imprint of Thomas Nelson. Elm Hill and Thomas Nelson are registered trademarks of HarperCollins Christian Publishing, Inc.

Elm Hill titles may be purchased in bulk for educational, business, fund-raising, or sales promotional use. For information, please e-mail SpecialMarkets@ ThomasNelson.com.

Scripture quotations marked ESV are from the ESV® Bible (The Holy Bible, English Standard Version®). Copyright © 2001 by Crossway, a publishing ministry of Good News Publishers. Used by permission. All rights reserved.

Scripture quotations marked MSG are from *The Message*. Copyright © by Eugene H. Peterson 1993, 1994, 1995, 1996, 2000, 2001, 2002. Used by permission of NavPress. All rights reserved. Represented by Tyndale House Publishers, Inc.

Scripture quotations marked NIV are from the Holy Bible, New International Version®, NIV®. Copyright © 1973, 1978, 1984, 2011 by Biblica, Inc.® Used by permission of Zondervan. All rights reserved worldwide. www.Zondervan.com. The "NIV" and "New International Version" are trademarks registered in the United States Patent and Trademark Office by Biblica, Inc.®

Scripture quotations marked NLT are from the Holy Bible, New Living Translation. © 1996, 2004, 2007, 2013, 2015 by Tyndale House Foundation. Used by permission of Tyndale House Publishers, Inc., Carol Stream, Illinois 60188. All rights reserved.

Library of Congress Cataloging-in-Publication Data

Prelaunch edition ISBN: 978-1-595557728

Library of Congress Control Number: 2018944793

ISBN 978-1-595557605 (Paperback)
ISBN 978-1-595557674 (Hardbound)
ISBN 978-1-595557681 (eBook)

About the Cover

You may be asking yourself why we picked a broken cup for the cover. This actually comes from a Japanese art form known as *Kinstugi*. In Japanese culture, broken objects are repaired with gold, lacquer, or platinum, which will highlight the broken flaw in the object. The Japanese do not see the brokenness of an object as detracting from an object's worth; instead, it is quite the opposite. They see the flaw as adding to the history and uniqueness of that piece, and it is seen as something to highlight rather than to hide. It honors the story and history of the object.

To me, this cup speaks volumes of my life. My pain, struggles, trials, failures, and sorrow are part of my story and, in hindsight, I have come to see them as being repaired and highlighted by the love of Jesus, which makes my story and your story valuable. Our stories are not something to hide or disguise, but rather to show the world so that the world can see the greatness of God's Love!

Cover design by Ben Kaiser

TRANSLATING *Love*

Michael Wogsland

Contents

About the Cover		*v*
Dedication		*xi*
Acknowledgments		*xiii*
Foreword		*xv*
Preface		*xvii*
Introduction		*xix*
1	The First Commandment	1
2	The Only Thing	7
3	The Key	13
4	A Powerful Truth	19
5	Not My Own	25
6	There is Only One	33
7	Learning to Hear	39
8	Our Worth	45
9	Unconditionally Unconditional	51
10	True Honor	59
11	The Will of the Father	67
12	What About You?	73
Final Thought		77
Notes		79
Meet the Man		81
About the Author		83

Dedication

This book is dedicated to my beautiful wife, Seira, and to our five amazing children.

My beautiful bride has supported me and stood by me when the rest of the world called me crazy. She prays for me, encourages me, lifts me when I am down, and pushes me to continually follow God and be the man He created me to be and to not give into my fears, worries, and self-doubts! She is my greatest gift and truly completes me!

And to my amazing children, who have been the biggest blessing from God to their mother and I and have been a driving force in all our work. They have stood with us in prayer even at a young age and have been a source of light and love in my life when things seemed darkest!

Acknowledgments

I would like to thank Hal Calisch for always being willing to take the time to show me these truths and for all partnering with me in support, wisdom, direction, and counsel in launching the Translating Love ministry!

I would like to thank John Newlin for his friendship, help and support, and the Newlin Chiropractic Clinic for doing everything possible to get me back on my feet!

I would like to thank my parents, Leonard and Kathy Wogsland, for their constant love and support and in their willingness to open their hands and release me by faith to follow the Lord's call on my life!

I would like to thank Scott and Dawn Brown for their friendship, encouragement. A huge thanks to everyone at Globe for putting up with me and helping me as I worked on this book. Especially Ben Kaiser for his amazing cover designs, and logos—you are awesome!

I would like to thank Liberty Church for their support of us in Japan. I would also like to thank the countless men and women who have helped with getting this book finished, and to the men of my advisory council for their direction—Thank you!

Foreword

Discipleship isn't a program, it's a person. It cannot be mass produced, because no one person is like another. It is this marvelous diversity that makes each person a prize worth winning back to our Father.

But who has time to spend on each person individually? God does.

Discipleship doesn't teach others to be like yourself, and it's not about teaching them your theology. It's about teaching them to relate to their Heavenly Father as the Messiah relates to Him. To receive, give, and walk in all of the love of the Father.

A good teacher must understand and love the subject they are teaching, and they must understand and love the person they are teaching.

~Hal Calisch

Preface

The purpose of this book is to encourage those who have ever felt like they have been beaten down by the world, by ministry, or by others. You may feel like you are spiraling out of control, have lost your footing, or simply have lost your waypoint and momentum.

This book is for people who may have at one time felt they knew their purpose and mission, and yet the realities of troubles in this world, the culture of comparison, and the spiritual attacks of the devil may have caused them to question whether they truly heard the will of God. Christ gives us a Great Commission with the objective to make disciples, and yet we feel inadequate in that because we may feel like we don't even know what it looks like to be a disciple. You may have asked or are even now asking yourself these questions: Do I truly have a purpose, and do I (my vision, my mission, and my life) truly matter?

Well. I wrote this book because the answer is a resounding **YES**! You are, and you do!

If I am honest, the reason you may not see that is that your perspective may be a little (or a lot) off. I know mine was! Your hearts' cry and desire, like mine, may be to hear the Divine One say, "Well done, my good and faithful servant." We feel ill-prepared and overwhelmed as we attempt to do the things God has laid on our hearts. We want to be faithful servants, trustworthy sons or daughters, and radical disciples, and yet we may have started to view this as an impossibility as we stare at the reality and potential futility of our efforts in our ministries, families, and lives. Is this sounding familiar? I know I can't be the only one.

Well, I have good news—no, GREAT NEWS! God-pleasing discipleship is not some hidden secret, mystic art form, or some lost step-by-step instruction manual that we need to accomplish before we can realize our potentials and destinies. Discipleship that will change the world and the course of our ministries and lives is learning how to translate and understand the love of God in our lives so that we can, in turn, express that love to others and by doing so, see their lives radically changed!

There is no step-by-step instruction manual for discipleship as true discipleship is unique to each person, but there are truths that God has revealed to us that will guide our way and will allow us to see and evaluate ourselves properly as we encounter and learn to translate the love of God. As we do this we will be faced with our shortcomings and errors, but if we yield to the truth and his love, we will be transformed to such an extent that we will begin to look like, smell like, talk like our teacher, master, Lord—Jesus Christ. This is discipleship, and this is achievable and necessary for all of God's children. For as we start to become him, we will be able to achieve the unique and special calling he has on all of our lives, which is to be disciples who make disciples who will change the world!

I pray that you will approach *Translating Love* with your ears, eyes, and hearts open. That you'd be willing to see the truths in these chapters and how they can apply to your life, and that you would allow God to do any heart work that is necessary or difficult.

Get ready for a wild ride, because once you have learned how to translate and understand God's love, it will radically affect everything you do and everyone you meet! I know this because it has happened to me!

INTRODUCTION

This book is nothing new, and yet everything new all at the same time. These truths came about as a result of a number of conversations between myself and a wonderful gentleman named Hal. From the very beginning of our relationship, I knew Hal was different—not a strange different, but different in a good way. In fact, I met the man at a bible study that I had been invited to, to share my testimony, and about a week after that, we set plans to meet up and get a coffee.

From that first meeting, Hal pulled no punches. He saw there were things in my life that were hindering me from moving forward in my relationship with God, and he, in essence, took a spiritual stick to my backside! Yet he did it in such a loving, caring way that I was open to receiving the correction. That one coffee shop meeting turned into many more, and every time Hal would never back down or shy around an issue, but rather he would lovingly lead me to confront an issue as he shined God's Word on the dark places of my heart and mind.

In hindsight, I believe I was receptive to this in part because I could tell he must care about me to risk our growing friendship by not letting me off the hook. Also in part because he had a very unique way of describing truths to me in ways that I had never heard before, and thus they were able to slip past my preprogrammed arguments and spiritual pride. They allowed me to ask difficult questions, wrestle with preconceived thoughts and behaviors, and conquer some areas of sin that I had glossed over because they didn't fall into the spectrum of the seven deadly sins, or so I thought!

During my time with Hal, his focus was on trying to call out the disciple of Christ in me by teaching me how to translate love. Before my time with Hal, I assumed that the love of God was one-dimensional. That the Love of God was one facet of God like mercy, goodness, kindness, even wrath. I knew that there were several different words in the Greek to describe love. There was brotherly love, passionate love, the love between a husband and wife love, and then pure or perfect love that was only capable by God. I had mistakenly assumed that love was quantifiable and identifiable by these four categories, and therefore anything that didn't fall into these categories was something other than love. As a result, there were areas of my life that became driven by argument, logic, experience, or my own personal feelings. I came to realize that I translated the events of my life through these filters.

In the beginning, as Hal and I continued to meet, I was frustrated in how he kept insisting that everything folded back into love. I couldn't understand why he kept insisting on it! Then one day as I was in my car I was thinking back to the time I picked out the diamond for my wife's engagement ring, and it was then that God revealed something to me. The diamond was the center point of the ring, and the quality and the cut of the diamond was important, as it would affect how light was refracted and reflected when people viewed the ring on my wife's finger. The diamond had many cuts and facets on it that made it shine, and the purity of the stone along with the precision of the cuts is what gave the diamond greater value. The same is true of God's love. The love of God is the diamond, and like a diamond, it has many "cuts and facets" to it as well. If we are willing and able to stand back and fully appreciate all of that in the love of God, it will change our perspective and worldviews, and may even radicalize us to actions that could change the world.

Translating Love is about learning how to see and understand the love of God in our lives so that we can, in turn, translate that love and share it with others. And in the process help them be able to understand and share that love with others as well.

I believe that a lot of what Hal taught me can help others as well, and that is why I am writing this book. What Hal taught was straight up scriptural, and yet he presented them in such a unique fashion that I felt compelled to record them to share with others. I hope and pray that you will not get hung up on my little labels or word choices. Instead, I hope and pray that you will be able to see and experience the Biblical truths of these statements in your life, and that you may too as I did find freedom and joy to tackle the vision and mission that God has given to you!

I should note as well about Hal in this book. I was trying to keep focused on what God was doing with me and didn't share the parts of the conversations where Hal detailed his struggles in learning these truths over a forty-year period. I am sorry if it comes across as if Hal magically had all the answers. He never preached at me; instead, he called out what he saw in me that was wrong because he had been there and showed me how God worked in his life—my arguments always came in when I wanted to see if his experiences or his truth lined up with scripture. I hope this helps clarify—thanks for your understanding!

CHAPTER 1

THE FIRST COMMANDMENT

So there I was standing in the entrance of a coffee shop as a broken, spiritually empty, heavily depressed, sciatica paralyzed, relatively young thirty-six-year-old missionary waiting to meet a man whom I had only met briefly a week or so earlier. I was mentally preparing myself and trying my best to put on a brave, confident, self-assured face because as a missionary every meeting is a potential partner for the work in the field. Nobody wants to collaborate with broken people, so I was working hard at pulling all the pieces together to portray a level of confident competency that I had lost a long time ago. I was broken spiritually, mentally, emotionally, and even physically.

I had been in the States now for about two months on my family's first furlough (think break) in nine years. My wife and I had started to see a counselor to begin untangling the mess we were in. In fact, the counselor diagnosed us with an emotional/mental disorder in the same category as PTSD but of lesser severity, and had ordered us to a mandatory three-month rest period, as we were struggling with everything that we had been through and, as a result, we weren't even thinking straight anymore. We had even lost the ability to have normal conversations between us—to say we were broken might be putting it lightly, it may be more accurate to say that we were destroyed or at least that is how it felt.

So how did we get to this place? Well, for nine years my family and I had been serving as missionaries in Japan. The first six years were in a little city in the south part of Osaka, and the last three years had been in the dead center of Kyoto, Japan, where we had been working on planting a church. Now most people when they hear about Kyoto think of a beautiful ancient city that is the pride of the Japanese nation. They think of the travel magazines that list Kyoto as the number one tourist destination in the world. They may think of Kyoto as the birthplace of Nintendo, or even as the city of the Gion Festival.

What is the Gion Festival, you may ask? It is one of the most famous Unesco World Heritage Festivals in the world celebrated for a month in Kyoto and attended by millions upon millions of people. Kyoto is a unique city of class, honor, history, art, sophistication, intelligence, and innovation!

But this is not what I see when I look at Kyoto. The Kyoto I know is the birthplace of Zen Buddhism and Shintoism, a city that is so steeped in religion that they have over 1600 Buddhist temples and 400 major Shinto shrines. A city that carries the moniker of the Missionaries Graveyard, and is the hardest mission field outside of the Middle East. A city where they say the son of Satan resides. This is the Kyoto that I know, and I was so naive going into it!

Since the age of four, I knew I had a calling from God to go to Kyoto, and growing up I fantasized about this city and what it must be like there, but boy was I wrong. The last three years there had been the hardest of my life, and it had pushed our fledgling ministry efforts, my family, and myself to the edge! Other missionaries and church leaders in Japan had warned me multiple times that Kyoto is where one goes to fail, and that I should direct my efforts elsewhere. We felt God calling us, and we pushed ahead but at a price. And now I identified myself as being broken, and this was my mindset as I waited to meet a man. A man named Hal.

Suddenly the bell on the coffee shop door chimed, and in walked Hal. Hal was a slim, average-height, messianic Jewish man who had made a name for himself in chiropractic consultations, and he had built a large chiropractic software company that served thousands of doctors and clinics nationwide. While he was the epitome of a successful businessman, his heart lay in ministry and ministering to others, and boy oh boy, was he good at it! We greeted each other cordially, got our coffee, and then sat down to talk.

Now because of my sciatica sitting was an extremely painful experience for me, but I was willing to endure for this meeting. I assumed that he would want to hear about our ministry and I would pitch him on the need and the opportunities for people to get involved with us, but to my surprise the conversation took a different twist. He had heard my testimony at the men's group a week or so earlier, so he was interested more in the now—where I was now spiritually, emotionally, and mentally.

We talked on a variety of subjects at length, and suddenly the conversation took an unexpected turn. Hal started addressing several of the areas in my life that I was struggling with. It was like he saw through my bravado and grandstanding and honed in on my secret struggles. He looked across the table at me and said, "Mike, something seems off—may I ask you a question?" This sudden and abrupt change in our conversation left me speechless for a moment but I managed a little nod, and he went on to ask a question. That question was the beginning of my journey in learning how to translate God's love. He said, "Mike, **have you ever thanked God FOR your pain, sickness, struggles, and failures? Because if you haven't you'll never move past where you are!**"

This question blew me away—thank God *for* my pain? *For* my struggles? *For* my failures? Is he crazy! I thank God *for* the good things like the miracles, the financial provision, and the successes I experience, but to thank him *for* my failures? That is just crazy—why should I thank God *for* my failures, *for* my pain, and *for* my struggles? I felt they were merely a reminder to me of how I had failed God and were in some part—such as in the cases of pain—a well-deserved punishment for my failings and for not being good enough, or in some cases even retribution for my sin.

Now I know that this is not the proper theology for a Christian to think, especially a pastor, and yet this is how I secretly felt. I had never voiced this or taught this, but this was my unspoken mindset. I mean who gives thanks *for* pain and sickness? I mean come on, we always pray for them to be taken away, for us to be healed and made whole. I have heard of giving thanks *in* times of trouble, and *in* times of struggle, and *in* times of pain, but whoever heard of giving thanks *for* them?

I really struggled with this; everything in me wanted to fight against it, but I was so broken that I knew my perspective needed to change. And it was then that I remember the verse found in Philippians 4:11–13: "Not that I was ever in need, for I have learned how to be content with whatever I have. I know how to live on almost nothing or with everything. I have learned the secret of living in every situation, whether it is with a full stomach or empty, with plenty or little. For I can do everything through Christ, who gives me strength." (NLT) And then I remembered what Paul said in 1 Thessalonians 5:16–18: "Be cheerful no matter what; pray all the time; thank God no matter what happens. This is the way God wants you who belong to Christ Jesus to live." (MSG) I realized I was not content, and that I was no longer thankful to God for everything. And this really opened my eyes.

After I left Hal, I went home and thought hard and long about what he said; in fact, I was so troubled that I could not remain still, so I grabbed a large walking staff and slowly begin to *hobble* my way around the neighborhood we were living in. As I shuffled along, I looked up into the sky and said, "Lord, I don't feel like thanking you for all the pain and the struggles and all the troubles, but I don't care how I feel! Lord, thank you for everything—for the pain of my childhood, for the troubles of my teenage years, and for the mess that I am currently in physically, spiritually, mentally, and emotionally. I thank you for all of it because, without all of it, I would not have seen you as active in my life, and now I want to live my life in a state of thankfulness—no longer dependent on my circumstances but rather I want it to be my lifestyle."

As I prayed this, a strange thing started to happen! Suddenly in the midst of my brokenness I begin to feel joy, not happiness. It was much stronger than happiness; it was a deeper emotion than happiness that could not be explained and could not be diminished, and it was then that I learned the secret that the apostle Paul was talking about!

The ***secret*** of contentment ***in*** all things was gratefulness *for* all things. In realizing this, something deep down in my heart started to change as I slowly began to understand the love of God in a way I had never known before. This would be the beginning of my healing, but there would be many more truths to follow that would truly liberate me from so much bondage as I began to learn how to translate and understand this thing called love.

Chapter 1 Verses to Consider:

"Not that I was ever in need, for I have learned how to be content with whatever I have. I know how to live on almost nothing or with everything. I have learned the secret of living in every situation, whether it is with a full stomach or empty, with plenty or little. For I can do everything through Christ, who gives me strength."

Philippians 4:11–13 (NLT)

"Be cheerful no matter what; pray all the time; thank God no matter what happens. This is the way God wants you who belong to Christ Jesus to live."

1 Thessalonians 5:16–18 (MSG)

"Do not be anxious about anything, but in every situation, by prayer and petition, with thanksgiving, present your requests to God."

Philippians 4:6 (NIV)

CHAPTER 2

THE ONLY THING

Well, about a month later Hal and I scheduled to meet up for another coffee. Hal had been in Jerusalem for a month and had just returned. I was still struggling with my Sciatic nerve issues, but I was actually looking forward to meeting up with Hal and hearing about his trip to Israel. Hal had felt led by God to go and seek him in Jerusalem for the next steps that Hal was to take, and so in obedience he had gone. I was curious to hear how it had gone, and if God had shown him anything yet. So a time was scheduled, and a date was set.

The day came and we met up at the coffee house again. I was truthfully surprised by how glad I was to see Hal, but upon further reflection I realized that it came from the deep-rooted respect that I had formed for the man. I had respected the fact that this man had risked a friendship with me to bring freedom and joy into my life by addressing a blind spot in my spiritual walk. This is a rare thing these days. Too often people care more about the friendship than they do the actual friend, to such an extreme that they won't address things with their friends that could save them from so much pain, all because they don't want to damage or threaten the idea of their friendship. This had not been my experience with Hal, and this is why I was looking forward to this meeting. I knew that I could trust him.

We got our coffees and went to sit outside—it was a nice warm morning, with a slight breeze. As we sat there sipping our hot Nicaraguan blend coffees, we exchanged pleasantries and then the conversation turned to his recent trip. I had so many questions! Where did he stay? Did he know what God wanted him to do for the next step? Did he meet anyone? Was he going to be moving to Jerusalem, etc.? During the conversation, Hal had expressed still a level of uncertainty in his next steps and told me that he had not received any clarity yet.

Hal sat quietly for a moment, then turned to me and asked, "Mike, what is the only thing that Jesus asks of you?" My mind started racing as I started looking for the proper biblical response. Eventually, I thought I had a good answer and said quite proud of myself, "To love the Lord God with all your heart, soul, mind and strength, and to love your neighbor as yourself." I could have sworn this was the proper response—I mean who is going to be able to say no to the greatest commandment! Well, I was about to find out who—and he was sitting across the table from me. He was about to introduce me to an important truth that would change my viewpoint forever.

"No, Mike. The only thing that Christ asks of us is *obedience*! And even then that obedience is a gift from him." This caught me completely off guard, and I quickly scrambled to analyze what he had just said and potentially come up with a counterargument. Now Hal must have seen this internal struggle play out on my face because he pressed me for my thoughts. I half mockingly laughed and said, "Well, that's a nice statement, but it doesn't play very well!" Hal looked at me inquisitively, so I continued, "Hal, come on! We live in a result-oriented world! No one is going to support a missionary that can't show results!"

Hal sat there with his elbows raised, hands folded under his chin, and looked out at the parking lot. Finally, he started to tell me a story of a friend of his.

"Mike, I have a friend who has been a missionary in Tunisia for thirty years. This man has suffered for the gospel and has faithfully shared the message of the gospel and the love of Christ for thirty years! One day I asked him how many people has he led to Christ in that time? Can you offer a guess, Mike?"

I started to open my mouth with a guess, and then I noticed him sitting there making a big zero with his hand.

"Let me help you, Mike—my friend told me after thirty years he could not show any results for his life of struggle, trial, and hardship in sharing the gospel to the people of Tunisia. So I asked him if he felt like had wasted his life and he said to me, 'Hal, I have been obedient to what God asked of me.'

"Now, Mike—would you consider him successful although he has no showable results?"

Instantly I thought back to the prophet Ezekiel where God promised the prophet that no one would listen to him, but that he was called to be a watchman for his people and that it was his job to still proclaim the warning to the people and to proclaim the prophecies that God would send. Was Ezekiel successful? Well, yes! He did what God called him to do, so I looked at Hal and nodded in affirmation as I said, "Yes, Hal, your friend is a success because he was obedient." In reply to this affirmation, Hal looked at me and said, "Well, then, what about you? Do you see yourself and your ministry in Kyoto as successful?"

This question hit me like a ton of bricks! Did I consider myself successful in the ministry in Kyoto? I didn't *feel* completely successful! In fact as I looked back over the last three years, I had mixed feelings. We had had financial struggles and trials with some huge breakthroughs. I had seen my "All-Star" ministry team implode, but I had also hosted and taken part in making history. Together with the first mission team that had come to help us, we became the first church in history allowed into the Buddhist-affiliated public schools in the center of Kyoto to share the love of Christ and to praise Him in a place where worship had never been lifted. This was huge because yearly the sacred child of the Gion festival is chosen from these schools. This simple action had made such an impact that a member from the Kyoto Board of education had remarked that they had never seen anything like this—families coming together, children dancing with parents, parents loving their children, and Jesus' name glorified!

I had not seen a great awakening and revival break out, but we had seen a small handful of people come to Christ. The average church in Japan might see one to two salvation decisions a year, and yet we had seen God move in calling more than a dozen to himself in our short time there. I remembered there were Sundays where I would preach to dozens and dozens of people and yet there were weeks I was literally preaching to one person. I remembered all the tears and prayers that we had prayed for people who needed miracles of healing in their lives and yet still died, and I remember all the tears and prayers that were answered with healings, salvations, and miracles. I remembered the feelings of complete helplessness and feeling completely overwhelmed by my insufficiencies and naïveté, and yet still I remembered the feelings of God taking control of a meeting and moving in ways that left me speechless.

Was this successful? If I was basing my success off results I might have ranked average, and yet as a missionary I felt the pressure to justify myself and the ministry by my results, and truthfully sometimes I didn't feel very successful! However, there was that question—was I validated by my results or by my obedience? Then I thought of John 14:15, "If you love me OBEY my commandments." As I thought on this, I recalled the story of Jesus talking to Peter after He had risen from the dead.

If you are not familiar with it, let me refresh your memory. After Jesus had risen from the dead, the disciples had decided to go fishing. They fished all night and caught nothing, and as the first rays of the morning light began to break the darkness of night, the disciples caught sight of a man on the shore. This man called to them and told them to cast their nets in one more time and, upon obeying him, they found their nets filled with fish! Peter realized who this was, and he leaped from the boat into the water and swam for shore. Upon reaching the shore, he found Jesus preparing some fish over a fire. Peter ran up to Jesus, and a conversation ensued. Now up until this point, the last thing Peter had in his memory bank was his triple layered betrayal and denial of Jesus. I can only assume that when Peter got to Jesus, a part of him was expecting and kind of hoping that Jesus would chew him out. He might have been hoping to make some sort of penance for his failures and betrayals, but Jesus flipped the script on him and asked the same question three times, "Peter, do you love me?" To which Peter inevitably replied in the positive, and then Jesus said this: "Then feed my sheep!"

It took me a moment, but then I got it! Jesus was not asking Peter for proof of his love by results, but rather by obedience. This realization then led to this thought: obedience is a gift from God that results in freedom. He gives us the ability to give up the right to determine and define what is successful and what is not, and the beauty here is we are left with freedom! Freedom to follow where Christ leads us and do what he tells us. And if we are obeying him in everything we say and do then we are successful, and we can leave the results up to him. Our goal is to one day hear God say, "Well done, my good and faithful servant!"

Upon reflecting on this, I turned to Hal and said, "I have done what Christ asked of me, and while I am struggling with my feelings on the results, I can say I have been obedient and thus I have been successful!"

While I had made a mental assent to this declaration, there was something unique in saying it aloud. It was as if as I was saying it, I felt like I was sowing purpose into me and my vision, my ministry, and my life.

Hal wasn't done yet: "Mike, there is still an important part to obedience that you need to grasp. It is only possible to please God when we are humble—it is impossible to please God when we are proud!"

What? There was a moment I was completely lost and couldn't figure out why Hal was bringing this up. "O-kay?" came my hesitant reply.

"I want to expand on this topic of obedience because this is crucial," Hal explained. It was then that Hal would blow me away with another truth. It would become crucial in helping me to understand love and in learning how to communicate that love to others.

"The only way we can please God in our obedience is by remaining humble, and do you know how you remain humble, Mike? You never take ownership!"

Chapter 2 Verses to Consider:

(Jesus): "If you love me, obey my commands."

JOHN 14:15 (NLT)

"Whoever has my commands and keeps them is the one who loves me. The one who loves me will be loved by my Father, and I too will love them and show myself to them."

JOHN 14:21 (NIV)

"Jesus replied, 'Anyone who loves me will obey my teaching. My Father will love them, and we will come to them and make our home with them.'"

JOHN 14:23 (NIV)

The story of Peter and Jesus - John 21

CHAPTER 3

THE KEY

What? What was this that Hal was trying to say? Inquisitively I asked Hal, "I'm sorry, Hal, could you repeat that?"

Hal looked at me and said, "Mike, it is only possible to please God when you're humble, and it's absolutely impossible to please God when you're proud."

I was confused. What was Hal trying to teach me with this? Why was this important to the topic we had just been discussing? How did this connect to the topic of obedience? My mind was racing as I was trying to simultaneously find answers to my questions and still contemplate what he had just said.

My length of silence must have been noticeable because Hal broke my silent contemplation by asking, "What are you thinking about?"

I looked sheepishly across the table and admitted, "Hal, I am not sure what this means and I'm confused about what you are trying to tell me!" In hindsight, I may have been a little blunt in saying this, but in the moment my brain wasn't computing. With the pain from my sciatic nerve wearing on my willpower and self-control, I was functioning at a bit less than optimal both in my ability to comprehend and in my ability to be civil. In truth, I fully expected Hal to take offense to this, but that was the exact opposite of what happened.

Looking kindly at me, he said, "To this point so far, we have been talking about obedience. Being obedient in anything and everything that the Messiah asks you to do. Now often we tend to lose sight of simply being obedient, and we start joining our identity to the task. Therefore the task becomes the most important thing as we allow it to become us. Then there is the added danger in that we start taking pride in our efforts of fulfilling the task which in turn bolsters our feelings of self-worth. Humility is key in preventing that because it is only possible to please God when you're humble and it is impossible to please God when you are proud!"

Wham! I felt like I had been mentally smacked awake with a wood plank and for a moment I lost awareness of my sciatic pain! He had in essence just identified me, and I knew it!

"Well, then, how do you stay humble?" I asked.

He smiled, replying: **"The key to staying humble is to never take ownership!"**

My mind was racing—what did he mean *by not taking ownership*? How were we to strive for excellence if we didn't take ownership? Even as that thought crossed my mind, I suddenly remembered the scripture verse that said, "And whatever your hand finds to do, do it heartily with all your strength as unto the Lord." Okay, I mentally conceded, but without ownership, I thought, there would seem to be no sense of urgency and no compelling reason to push the envelope? This was all so confusing!

Suddenly I felt the sciatic pain that I had forgotten about a moment earlier come rushing back with full force, and so I told Hal I needed some time to think about this. I think he could see my rising physical discomfort and agreed, and so we said our good byes and parted ways.

Hal's words stuck with me and I continued to ponder them but with growing confusion. I knew in my heart the truth of what he was saying *about* humility, but it would take a conversation a few weeks later that would really define for me *what* humility was. I still was having trouble being able to fully grasp it and apply it to my life. If I were honest, I was still struggling with the ownership idea.

Well, a few weeks later Hal decided to drive a friend's dog from Florida to California. On the first day of the trip, I called Hal to check up on his progress and see how he was doing. A few moments into the conversation, Hal redirected the topic and asked about our previous conversation on *humility*. "Have you given any thought to our previous conversation about living in humility by never taking ownership?"

Feeling a bit chagrined, I hesitantly admitted to Hal that I was actually really confused about it and that I was struggling with the idea of never taking ownership. "Could you explain it a bit more to me?" I sheepishly asked. Hal's response was so quintessentially Hal: "I'd love to, Mike!"

Hal, ever the ready teacher started off with a bang! "Mike, the key question in all this hinges on the question of who is on the throne. True humility is about having God occupy the throne rather than trying to occupy it ourselves!"

My mind was racing to keep up, but so far I agreed.

Hal continued, "We need to seek the will of God in everything! So often we see opportunities to do good, and we assume that is what God wants us to do. We make the judgment call based on our evaluation of good in the situation. We need to stop seeking to do good, but rather we need to be seeking the One who is good! Humility is not taking for granted what we do right. Our heart has to be bowed! When I am acting out of pride, it is many things but not bowed. Bowing the heart is more significant than bowing the knee—it is bowing your very essence! Our example is the Messiah; He only went to places, said things, did miracles that God the Father told him to. Do our actions look like his? What's more is that pride is the hiding of your true self from God, yourself, and others. It is necessary when the real you falls short of your own expectations. We hide behind a false image that is practically perfect and is above reproach. However, the Messiah did not die for the image, so the image cannot please God. This is so sad! Many of us labor under pride to some degree. Humility, on the other hand, ditches all pretense and stands in truth before God, who gladly accepts the real person, warts and all, because the Messiah died for one such as this."

Suddenly it was as if someone had turned on a lightbulb in the dark basement of my mind! What I had found so confusing before was now clear. Humility to me had always been defined as "Not thinking less of yourself, but thinking of yourself less." I had always struggled with this because my pride was so quick in situations, but here I realized that my problem with *humility* was that my pride and I were still in the picture. I was still making an evaluation of myself, of my situation, my actions, and my successes and failures. I was still taking ownership and not giving my true self entirely over to the Messiah!

Even as this thought crossed my mind I shuddered as I thought back to all the times I had elevated myself by doing things because they appeared good, they made me feel good, or they made me look good. How much of my ministry, my life had I been taking ownership of? How much of it had been done out of pride and ego, and how much of it had truly brought glory to God?

The gravity of this realization was sobering, and as I sat there I started to think back on so many experiences and scenarios where I could see that I had done things because I had said they were good, or because the world or at the very least the Christian community would think so. I thought back to feeding the homeless, to doing outreach activities, to even preaching messages where I had done these things from if not a position of pride, at the very least from a position of self-gratification because doing good made me feel or look good! Had I done any good? Had the majority of my life and work been a waste?

These thoughts were crushing me!

"Oh, God!" I prayed. "Forgive me for trying to occupy your throne! Forgive me for taking ownership and elevating my own evaluations above you. Help me, Lord, to simply follow you in obedience in all situations. I will go wherever and do whatever you desire! I am bare before you; you see the real me—redeem my life and thank you for redeeming me!"

Even as my world came crashing down around me, the Lord in his mercy reminded me once again it was not my place to occupy the throne and evaluate the worth of my actions to God. I was reminded that God can redeem and that there is no condemnation in Christ to those who love God and are called according to his purpose.

This revelation of humility in obedience changed everything for me! It changed my perspective and my focus. It gave me the freedom to follow, the strength to obey, and the courage to stand in the realization of my obedience to the One who is on the throne. For now, the truth of Galatians 2:20 came alive to me: "My old self has been crucified with Christ. It is no longer I who lives, but Christ who lives in me. So I live in this earthly body by trusting in the Son of God, who loved me and gave himself for me."

Chapter 3 Verses to Consider:

"Whatever you do, work heartily, as for the Lord and not for men."

COLOSSIANS 3:23 (ESV)

"Do nothing from selfish ambition or conceit, but in humility count others more significant than yourselves. Let each of you look not only to his own interests, but also to the interests of others. Have this mind among yourselves, which is yours in Christ Jesus, who, though he was in the form of God, did not count equality with God a thing to be grasped, but emptied himself, by taking the form of a servant, being born in the likeness of men. And being found in human form, he humbled himself by becoming obedient to the point of death, even death on a cross. Therefore God has highly exalted him and bestowed on him the name that is above every name, so that at the name of Jesus every knee should bow, in heaven and on earth and under the earth, and every tongue confess that Jesus Christ is Lord, to the glory of God the Father."

PHILIPPIANS 2:3–11 (ESV)

"The Lord has told you what is good, and this is what he requires of you: to do what is right, to love mercy, and to walk humbly with your God."

MICAH 6:8 (NLT)

"My old self has been crucified with Christ. It is no longer I who lives, but Christ who lives in me. So I live in this earthly body by trusting in the Son of God, who loved me and gave himself for me."

GALATIANS 2:20

CHAPTER 4

A Powerful Truth

With a heavy sigh I pushed open the door of the chiropractic clinic and made my way to the car in the parking lot. I was going to meet up with Hal for our coffee get-together, but I was really struggling. I was struggling first with intense back pain and from some depressing news that I had just heard. While in the chiropractic office the chiropractor, a very talented young lady, had been informing me that after several months of treatment, my spine was now in full alignment. However, because I was still in incredible pain, she informed me that I had either slipped a disc in my spine or that I had a herniated disc—both of which would result in putting pressure on my sciatic nerve and were making even the smallest movements for me so painful.

I was sick of pain—I was trying to manage it with painkillers and minimal movements, but even limiting my movements did not help because the simplest action like going to the restroom or turning on my side in the bed caused my back to be in extreme pain. If I were on a good day the pain would be slightly manageable, but by about two in the afternoon the constant pain would have so eroded my willpower that the slightest thing sent me into an emotional tailspin and I was beginning to have a problem with my anger. I was angry that I could not play with kids, let alone hug them. I was angry that every moment of my time was consumed with bearing with the pain. I began to loathe even the simplest of actions like getting out of bed because the pain would grip me in such a tight fashion a second felt like an hour and a minute felt like a day, and a day felt like an eternity. There was no escaping this pain, and I was feeling trapped! Then I got this news—my spine was in alignment, so it must be a disc problem!

I was crushed! We had discussed my options, but there were no good options. The first option was to get some steroid shots but they were $5000 apiece, and I was a poor missionary with no insurance in the States. The second option was no better—back surgery. Again, poor missionary with no insurance! I felt trapped in this world of pain, and as I slowly, painfully lowered myself into the Nissan Pathfinder we had been lent by a local church, my hope and faith almost gave out! I couldn't take it anymore, but I was going to hold it together a little bit longer because of my meeting with Hal.

I arrived at the coffee shop and I could see that Hal was already there, sitting at this little table outside the coffee shop that had become *our* spot. I slowly got out of the car and, with my Moses-style walking stick that I had been using, I slowly made my way over to him. We greeted each other, went inside to get our coffees, and then made our way back out to our spot. Once I had slowly lowered myself into the chair, Hal opened the conversation by asking about my chiropractic appointment. I was in dark place as I recounted for Hal what the chiropractor had told me and what my options were. Things seemed hopeless: I was going to have to resign myself to living in pain.

Hal surprised me though by suddenly speaking out, "Mike, I disagree! The healing you need is spiritual, not physical!"

I looked at him in surprise! Excuse me?! Did he not see that the pain I was in was physical? This was a problem with actual physical pain and didn't have anything to do with joy or obedience. Maybe I had heard him wrong. Hal seemed to be able to read my thoughts though, because he repeated what he had just said, "Mike, listen to me—the healing you need is spiritual, not physical."

A Powerful Truth

I responded with a level of incredulity, "What do you mean?"

His response only increased my level of incredulity. "Something still seems off in you spiritually. So let me ask you this question: do you feel blame, pressure, or condemnation when you think of your ministry in Japan?"

This line of questioning had caught me off guard, so I responded snarkily, "Sure, yeah—what missionary doesn't?"

He looked me dead in the eye as he said, "There's your problem: you need to repent!"

BOOM! It was as if I had been hit with a super punch out of a video game, and it had me reeling! Repent?! What was he talking about? Hal had never been this direct in calling for me to repent before, and this along with my pain had me on the defensive.

"What are you talking about?" I frustratingly asked.

That is when Hal blew my world apart with another truth.

"Mike, you can't take the blame without secretly wanting the credit. If you're willing to accept the blame, struggles, and condemnation of others with regards to your ministry, that means you are also willing to accept and take credit for any of the successes you might have had too!

That is spiritual pride! Remember God has called you to obedience, and even then it is a gift from him!"

This revelation stopped me dead in my tracks! This truth had hit a bull's-eye! I had never thought of it that way before. I had never thought that by feeling a sense of ownership to perceived blame, pressure, and condemnation that I was being prideful, and yet as I thought about this more, I began to realize how true it was.

Inside one of my deepest places, I had secretly fantasized about being the missionary who would bring about a great awakening to the Japanese nation. A nation considered the second largest unreached population group in the world, and a nation that had historically been very closed to the Gospel.

I had felt called to Japan since I was four years old, and I had seen God bring me back to life on an operating table where I was having surgery on a level-4 malignant brain tumor. I had died during that operation, but God had brought me back to life! I had been blind, and God had healed my eyesight. I had shattered my skull into my brain, and God had sent an angel to heal me completely within sixteen hours. I was even the oldest living survivor in the world, after having an experimental Shunt tube break in me after being dependent on it for years. I was a miracle, and I had always been told that God had big plans for my life.

While I had never voiced it, I had always assumed the Japanese nation was merely waiting for my arrival for them to turn to Jesus. I was going to be known as the missionary who did it! And as I write this now, I can hear the ludicrousness of my arrogance, and yes, if I were to be honest, I had truthfully expected it, and when it didn't happen like I had assumed it would, it had depressed me!

In this depressed mindset, I had thought it was humble of me to take the full blame for the lack of a great spiritual awakening in Japan, and yes, I felt the condemnation of the Church as a whole because I had not been the white knight who had saved the day. I assumed my struggles were a brand to be worn as one who was not spiritually, physically, mentally, or emotionally different from any other "failed" missionary who had gone before me! I literally quantified myself and justified my time and efforts in Japan by my struggles and pain, and I thought this was the ultimate in humility! Boy, was I wrong! For the first time, I saw it for what it really was—PRIDE! And boy oh boy, was it ugly!

The rest of the day seemed to pass in a haze as my mind kept turning over and over the words of Hal. By the time I lowered myself painfully into bed that night, I was broken! As I lay there in pain, I started to cry and call out to God! I asked him to forgive me for my spiritual pride, for my false humility, and for trying to own things that were not mine to own! I asked God to forgive me for losing sight of him, and I asked him for the strength to release the feelings of ownership I had acquired for the blame, struggles, and the condemnation that I felt.

I am not sure how long I prayed, only that I prayed until I fell asleep, and the next thing I remembered was waking up the following morning and reaching for the stick and little assist thing I used for getting out of bed. As I reached for it, I suddenly realized that I wasn't feeling any pain! This sudden thought surprised me, and I sat up in bed.

I sat up in bed?!

There had been no pain! I swung my legs slowly out of bed and gingerly stood to my feet—without the use of any device to aid me. There was no pain! I started to walk a bit and got to the step leading from our bedroom into the kid's room/living room. Again, there was a surprising absence of pain! With each step, my confidence grew—not just in my newfound healing, but also in the realization of the freedom that God had shown me! I was free from all the feelings of condemnation and blame. I felt light and joyful! I quickly woke my wife and children to declare the wonderful news! I was better not just physically but also spiritually! Oh, the freedom from the physical pain was so sweet, but the freedom from the burdensome load of false humility and pride was sweeter still!

It was then that a scripture verse came to my mind and I love how it is voiced in the message bible: "For my part, I am going to boast about nothing but the Cross of our Master, Jesus Christ. Because of that Cross, I have been crucified in relation to the world, set free from the stifling atmosphere of pleasing others and fitting into the little patterns that they dictate. Can't you see the central issue in all this? It is not what you and I do—submit to circumcision, reject circumcision. It is what God is doing, and he is creating something totally new, a free life! All who walk by this standard are the true Israel of God—his chosen people. Peace and mercy on them!" Galatians 6:14-16 MSG

Oh, the Freedom!

Chapter 4 Verses to Consider:

"For my part, I am going to boast about nothing but the Cross of our Master, Jesus Christ. Because of that Cross, I have been crucified in relation to the world, set free from the stifling atmosphere of pleasing others and fitting into the little patterns that they dictate. Can't you see the central issue in all this? It is not what you and I do—submit to circumcision, reject circumcision. It is what God is doing, and he is creating something totally new, a free life! All who walk by this standard are the true Israel of God—his chosen people. Peace and mercy on them!"

GALATIANS 6:14–16 (MSG)

"Do nothing from selfish ambition or conceit, but in humility count others more significant than yourselves."

PHILIPPIANS 2:3 (ESV)

"I hope in the Lord Jesus to send Timothy to you soon, so that I too may be cheered by news of you. For I have no one like him, who will be genuinely concerned for your welfare. For they all seek their own interests, not those of Jesus Christ. But you know Timothy's proven worth, how as a son with a father he has served with me in the gospel."

PHILIPPIANS 2:3, 19–22 (ESV)

CHAPTER 5

NOT MY OWN

Since the age of four, I had been convinced that God had shared six truths about my life with me. I knew these six things like I knew the answer to 2 + 2. There had never been a question about these six things in my life. I knew:

1.) I was never going to date.
2.) I was going to marry a Japanese girl.
3.) I was going to be a pastor.
4.) I was going to live in Japan.
5.) I was going to be a pastor in Kyoto.
6.) I was going to bring good news to the Japanese people.

In fact, I was so convinced of this that as a young child I had circled the city of Kyoto on a map and had said, "This is my city!" And throughout the years God in his miraculous wisdom and mercy brought each one of these things to pass in my life.

My life had been mapped out for me, and my identity was Mike from Japan. And yet I was at a major crossroads in my life that found me struggling with my identity and ministry, and knowing that any decision I would make would impact not just myself but my family and many others. This was the dilemma I was in as I sat in our usual spot in the coffee shop talking with Hal. I was struggling but trying hard not to show it.

Hal and I had been talking for about 30 minutes on the previously explored topic of obedience when Hal suddenly brought up an interesting question. "Mike, as you serve in Japan, whose ministry is it?" I paused for a minute before answering.

"Well, I know what you're gonna say, Hal, but for the sake of the conversation I will bite—it's mine." I thought I knew where Hal was going to take this. I mean we had previously talked about humility, obedience, and the importance of not taking ownership, so when he asked I thought we would be rehashing that conversation, and yet that is not what Hal had in mind!

Hal was sitting with his legs crossed taking a drink from his cup of Colombian brewed coffee. Setting his cup down he looked at me, smiled, and said, "Well, then, what if the Messiah asked you to give it up?"

I felt a cold shiver run down my spine as I looked at him with my mouth gaping open. How did Hal know? Just the other night my wife and I had taken our kids to a local park at the library and had been discussing the predicament that we were in. Recently we saw roughly about 80 percent of our committed support dry up due to a number of different circumstances. As a result, my wife and I had been presented with some very real difficulties, and we didn't know what to do. We were feeling depressed and trapped. There didn't seem to be any good solutions—at least that was until I remembered a suggestion from my friend, Scott.

Scott was one of my best friends in the whole world, and he had the added benefit of looking like Tony Stark from the movie *Iron Man*. He had suggested that we do a complete ministry relaunch, and at the time I had laughed it off as a crazy idea because it had been so hard the first time getting into Kyoto that I couldn't imagine the idea of trying to do it again.

Yet as my wife and I discussed our situation, it seemed like the only healthy option available to us was one that I couldn't fathom making.

Kyoto was my destiny! Kyoto was my identity! Yet, Hal had just asked the question that was heaviest on my heart!

"Why would he do that, Hal?" came my fiery response. "He called me to Kyoto, why would he call me to give it up? He gave me a twenty-year vision, he provided the money to go to Kyoto, and this has been a lifetime in the making! In Japan I am known as Pastor Mike (actually Mike- Sensei), and in America I was regularly referred to as Mike the missionary to Kyoto. What am I if I leave? My heart and desires lie in Kyoto, why take it away? On top of that, Kyoto is one of the hardest mission fields in the world, and my wife and I were planting the only church (at that time) in the center of the city. Why would God ask us to stop such necessary work and come back to America?

Hal took another drink of his coffee before giving me a truth that would completely undo me and change my perspective: **"A devoted person doesn't own his own life."**

This was sounding a lot like the humility topic about never taking the ownership, but Hal meant something much more profound.

"Mike, you're identity needs to be in Christ alone. Anything outside of that is pride and is wrong! The Master has every right to tell the servant where to go and what to do. It may not be what the servant wants, but it is what the Master wants because only the master understands the why!"

I knew I had to agree with Hal because he was speaking the truth, but it still didn't help. I still wanted an answer to my question: WHY?

I would continue to struggle with this question throughout the day. The longer I thought about it, the more depressed I became.

Later that evening, my wife and I went out to dinner with Scott and his wife, Dawn. As soon as we sat down, Scott asked us how we were doing. We opened up and shared everything that was going on in our lives. We felt so frustrated, but as we sat there sharing, Scott's beautiful wife, Dawn, spoke up.

"Mike, this is so exciting! Just think back to Abraham. He had been given a promise—it was a promise that would lead to Abraham's mission of being a blessing to all nations and that promise was his son Isaac. Now

Abraham waited until he was a hundred years old for that promise to be recognized. And once it was, God came and asked Abraham to give it up. God asked Abraham to lay it on an altar and sacrifice it back to God. God wanted to see if he was willing to give it back to him. He wanted to see if He was still the most important thing to Abraham. God may be asking the same of you, Mike!"

As she said this, my conversation with Hal came rushing back! I realized that God was asking me if I was truly devoted. I didn't need the why: I just needed to trust in the wisdom, love, and character of the master. God wanted my identity to be in Christ alone and nothing else. As soon as I realized this, the answer to the question of what should we do became very clear, and we had the courage and grace to make it! For now, I truly understood what it meant to be a devoted man.

After going home that night, my wife and I went for a walk in the neighborhood and talked about everything. Together we prayed one of the hardest prayers of our lives! We laid it all down on the altar, and the strangest thing happened: we felt peace! Peace in knowing that God was in control! Peace in knowing that God loves the Japanese more than my wife and I, and that he also loved us and would be working all things out for his glory and our good! Wow! As we realized this, joy started to build in us! We no longer felt trapped or depressed; instead, we were filled with courage, joy, and hope for the future! What a wonderful thing to trust your future and purpose into the hands of the One who owns it all! We no longer needed to seek the whys, we just need to follow him wherever he may lead!

Chapter 5 Verses to Consider:

"And whatever you do, in word or deed, do everything in the name of the Lord Jesus, giving thanks to God the Father through him."

Colossians 3:17 (ESV)

"So here's what I want you to do, God helping you: Take your everyday, ordinary life—your sleeping, eating, going-to-work, and walking-around life—and place it before God as an offering. Embracing what God does for you is the best thing you can do for him. Don't become so well-adjusted to your culture that you fit into it without even thinking. Instead, fix your attention on God. You'll be changed from the inside out. Readily recognize what he wants from you, and quickly respond to it. Unlike the culture around you, always dragging you down to its level of immaturity, God brings the best out of you, develops well-formed maturity in you."

Romans 12:1-2 (MSG)

"I appeal to you therefore, brothers, by the mercies of God, to present your bodies as a living sacrifice, holy and acceptable to God, which is your spiritual worship. Do not be conformed to this world, but be transformed by the renewal of your mind, that by testing you may discern what is the will of God, what is good and acceptable and perfect."

Romans 12:1-2 (ESV)

"Some time later, God tested Abraham's faith. 'Abraham!' God called. 'Yes,' he replied. 'Here I am.' 'Take your son, your only son—yes, Isaac, whom you love so much—and go to the land of Moriah. Go and sacrifice him as a burnt offering on one of the mountains, which I will show you.' The next morning Abraham got up early. He saddled his donkey and took two of his servants with him, along with his son, Isaac. Then he chopped wood for a fire for a burnt offering and set out for the place God had told him about. On the third day of their journey, Abraham looked up and saw the place in the distance. 'Stay here with the donkey,' Abraham told the servants. 'The boy and I will travel a little farther. We will worship there, and then we will come right back.' So Abraham placed the wood for the burnt offering on Isaac's shoulders, while he himself carried the fire and the knife. As the two of them walked on together, Isaac turned to Abraham and said, 'Father?' 'Yes, my son?' Abraham replied. 'We have the fire and the wood,' the boy said, 'but where is the sheep for the burnt offering?' 'God will provide a sheep for the burnt offering, my son,' Abraham answered. And they both walked on together. When they arrived at the place where God had told him to go, Abraham built an altar and arranged the wood on it. Then he tied his son, Isaac, and laid him on the altar on top of the wood. And Abraham picked up the knife to kill his son as a sacrifice. At that moment the angel of the Lord called to him from heaven, 'Abraham! Abraham!' 'Yes,' Abraham replied. 'Here I am!' 'Don't lay a hand on the boy!' the angel said. 'Do not hurt him in any way, for now I know that you truly fear God. You have not withheld from me even your son, your only son.' Then Abraham looked up and saw a ram caught by its horns in a thicket. So he took the ram and sacrificed it as a burnt offering in place of his son. Abraham named the place Yahweh-Yireh (which means "the Lord will provide"). To this day, people still use that name as a proverb: 'On the mountain of the Lord it will be provided.' Then the angel of the Lord called again to Abraham from heaven. 'This is what the Lord says: Because you have obeyed me and have not withheld even your son, your only son, I swear by my own name that I will certainly bless you. I will multiply your descendants beyond number, like the stars in the sky and the sand on the seashore. Your descendants will conquer the cities of their enemies. And through your descendants all the nations of the earth will be blessed—all because you have obeyed me.'"

GENESIS 22:1–18 (NLT)

CHAPTER 6

THERE IS ONLY ONE

Hal had been in Israel for several weeks now, and we had been keeping in touch via Facebook Messenger. On this particular day, we had been having a lively conversation on a number of different topics, but things were getting interesting as we discussed discipleship!

A discipler must so own the attitudes he or she is trying to pass on. We must be Messianic: that is, we must own the traits of the Messiah. These traits are contagious. Hal Wrote.

This message had captured my thoughts –

How do we do that? I quickly replied.

Well, we have already talked about obedience, so an effective discipler is an obedient disciple. And the key to being a good disciple is to obey whatever the Master tells you!

This is good—this was something that I could sink my teeth into!

Finally, I thought to myself. This will be a conversation about a theory of practice—I enjoyed these conversations as they rarely required commitment, but instead I found them to be a fun exercise in critical thinking and theory.

And yet this was not Hal's intent, and it was as if he could see through my arguments and ideas as easily as someone ripping wet toilet paper. So to get me back on track, Hal was about to destroy my mind games with another spiritual truth.

Mike, a good disciple should be the Messiah!

Wait! What was this?

My response was almost instantaneous

Ummm, I'm sorry: could you clarify that?

It was amazing to me how quickly my defenses went up in response to this simple statement. To me, what he had just written sounded a little cultish. Be the Messiah? There is only one Messiah, and His name is Jesus! Be the Messiah? What was he saying? Were we to worship ourselves as saviors of the world?

Hal's response was taking a few minutes to come back as he was typing and as the time ticked on by, I got more and more wound up. I began thinking of all the rebuttals and verses that I could use; I started laying out a strategy of defensive arguments along with a proactive game plan for convincing Hal he had crossed the line! I was gonna win this for the sake of his soul, I told myself! Determination and righteous indignation were fueling my thoughts and running through my veins.

Then, in an instant, my righteous indignation was gone when I read the next thing Hal sent.

Have you ever considered what Jesus said in John 14:6—where he said he is the Way, the Truth, and the Life? Jesus made the way by his death on the cross, and then he sent the helper to us to instruct us in all truth so that we may live in him, by him, and through him. The One we are to be is the whole point. Not very complicated, but nuanced perhaps. HE is the Kingdom. We are to be HIM, not like Him, not inspired by Him. BE HIM. We do that by only doing what He tells us to do.

That is a beautiful thought, I thought to myself, but the reality is another thing. I mean Christ was perfect, and he didn't struggle with a sin nature! While I, on the other hand, struggled all the time with my anger, lust, pride, and many numbers of different things.

My mind was racing as I started to tear into what he was saying. Was this even possible?

It was then that I thought of the verse in Colossians 3:1–4 where it says, "Since you have been raised to new life with Christ, set your sights on the realities of heaven, where Christ sits in the place of honor at God's right hand. Think about the things of heaven, not the things of earth. For you died to this life, and your real life is hidden with Christ in God. And when Christ, who is your life, is revealed to the whole world, you will share in all his glory."

I found this verse really convicting and yet I continued to struggle with this for several weeks. I couldn't comprehend how this could be an expected reality. I was so imperfect! The Messiah was the definition of perfection! In my mind I could not reconcile these two thoughts, and I found the very thought of it depressing. Depressing because if the goal was perfection, I wasn't even on the scoreboard and I didn't have any hope of being that way, so I felt like I should just resign myself to failure.

So during another get-together with Hal after he had gotten back from Israel, I decided to broach the topic again.

"Hal, what did you mean by be the Messiah?" I asked. "How is that even possible?"

Hal looked at me and smiled. "One minute at a time."

I think Hal could see the incredulity and annoyance on my face at this answer, so he continued. "Mike, it starts minute by minute, then ten minutes, an hour, a half of day, a day, then two till it becomes a way of life. Think of it as maturing. A baby doesn't stay a baby; first, he learns to crawl, then stand, then walk—eventually they change into a toddler, then a young boy or girl, then a teenager, then an adult. It is a progression. A baby is not expected to be able to do what an adult does, but an adult shouldn't be still acting like a baby. This is the same way we are to be the Messiah!"

OK, I thought, but then another question hit me. "So is this all works-based—is it all dependent on my doing good things in a godly way? And even then this doesn't negate my sin nature, so how can I be perfect like the Messiah?"

"It's not about you," Hal said kindly. "It is about Him! He is preparing us as His bride, and you know what will please him? A bride that He prepares that He pursues that He wins for Himself. And a bride that is so in love with Him that they are willing to give up everything for Him, even their identity!"

This truth knocked me back into my seat! As I started to contemplate it more and more, I began to get excited. I realized that in and of myself I was incapable of being what God demanded, but through the Messiah and His work on my behalf—both in me and through me—he would be faithful to create in me what would best please him. I simply needed the mind of Christ, and that was something that He was more than willing to give because He loved me and because I was part of His bride!

I left that meeting with a spring in my step, realizing the faithfulness of Jesus to His plans and His desires. It gave me hope because I was part of them. It allowed me the courage to pray, "Lord help me to completely lose myself in you, that the world no longer sees me, Lord, but that they simply see you when they look at me! Give me your mind, your heart, your love, and your strength every moment, Lord. Help me to start resembling you in every part of my life."

Now I understood what Hal had been trying to say—Jesus' desire for us is to be the Messiah—to be hid in Him so that the world through us might know Him! Now I can say out of complete humility, with fear and trembling, that as a disciple, I am to be the Messiah.

Chapter 6 Verses to Consider:

"And those who belong to Christ Jesus have crucified the flesh with its passions and desires. If we live by the Spirit, let us also keep in step with the Spirit."

Galatians 5:24–25 (ESV)

"Husbands, love your wives, as Christ loved the church and gave himself up for her, that he might sanctify her, having cleansed her by the washing of water with the word, so that he might present the church to himself in splendor, without spot or wrinkle or any such thing, that she might be holy and without blemish."

Ephesians 5:25–27 (ESV)

"Since you have been raised to new life with Christ, set your sights on the realities of heaven, where Christ sits in the place of honor at God's right hand. Think about the things of heaven, not the things of earth. For you died to this life, and your real life is hidden with Christ in God. And when Christ, who is your life, is revealed to the whole world, you will share in all his glory."

Colossians 3:1–4 (NLT)

"Jesus told him, "I am the way, the truth, and the life. No one can come to the Father except through me."

John 14:6 (NLT)

CHAPTER 7

LEARNING TO HEAR

It was a gloomy day. The clouds had burst like a pipe and there had been a constant, nonstop drizzle of rain for the last three days! It was the kind of weather that makes you want to stay home, get back into bed, and sleep until the sun reappears. That is not where I was, though, as I was sitting inside the coffee shop waiting for Hal to arrive. As gloomy as the weather was outside, it was even worse in my mind. My wife and I had been struggling with the ramifications of our decision to do a complete ministry relaunch. This decision was weighing heavily on us, and we were second-guessing ourselves now in everything. This led to more stress and even to disagreements and some small fights. We felt like we were in a boat that had lost its ability to navigate and steer, and it was resulting in fear. The fear was becoming debilitating. This was my mindset and mood when I received the little Facebook message about meeting up with Hal for coffee.

The door chimed and in walked Hal. We greeted each other with a hug and went to order our coffee. After getting our Sumatran coffees, we sat down and started catching up. Hal and I hadn't met up for a while, and so we talked at length on a number of topics. As usual, Hal seemed to hone in on the part of me that I was struggling with, so he asked, "Mike, you seem like you are weighed down with something big. Are you struggling with fear?"

I was shocked! Could he really read me so easily? "Yeah, a bit," was my terse reply.

Hal sat back for a moment with his hands folded under his chin, and his eyes closed. A part of me was worried that my abrupt reply would be taken as an angry outburst, but that thought was proved false as soon as Hal spoke.

Opening his eyes, He looked at me and asked a question that completely threw me off my game. "How do you hear God, Mike?"

What? Where did this question come from? I was super confused, but I racked my brain for an answer. Usually I didn't struggle with this kind of question, as I had counseled dozens and dozens of people in the past on this very thing. For some reason, though, the abruptness of this question along with the sudden change in the conversation had rendered me momentarily speechless. The very fact that I was speechless was infuriating to me as I should've known the answer to this question automatically.

Haltingly and yet trying to add bravado to my voice to overcome my insecurity at finding that I had nothing to say—as I was simply pulling a blank—I started hemming and hawing to gain some time for my brain to kick into gear!

"Well, you know—it's like you just know." Came my pitiful answer.

Hal just looked at me, and I realized he was giving me time to think about it. So I continued to speak out, hoping it would jumpstart my train of thought. Try as hard as I might, I could only pull how we can know we have an assurance of salvation. So I thought, *That sounds spiritual, I'll just go with that!* "The Word, Our Testimony, and the Holy Spirit," I continued, albeit somewhat embarrassingly.

I could see Hal was not biting at these Christianese answers, and yet I realized that he was not a man who ever spoke without reason. So finally I gave up and asked him, "Okay, Hal, I can't think straight right now, so help me out here. How do we hear God?"

Hal leaned over the table and said to me, "Mike, **the number one key to hearing God is knowing how much you're loved!** If you are struggling to hear God, it is because you are struggling with his love."

This hit my fear and me like the force of a tomahawk missile leveling a building. Suddenly a verse popped into my mind: "Such love has no fear because perfect love expels all fear. If we are afraid, it is for fear of punishment, and this shows that we have not fully experienced his perfect love." 1 John 4:18 NLT

Hal's words had struck a nerve, and like a nerve that is pinched, I couldn't ignore it!

I would continue to contemplate Hal's words throughout the day—"The number one key to hearing God is knowing how much you're loved! If you are struggling to hear God, it is because you are struggling with his love."

I mean I knew God loved me. I grew up singing the famous Sunday school song, "Jesus loves me this I know for the Bible tells me so...." Did I doubt his love? Was that why I was so fearful? As if in answer to my questions, I suddenly thought back to the decision my wife and I had recently made with doing a ministry relaunch. To me, I understood that all Jesus was asking of me was obedience and even then following him in obedience was a gift from him. I realized that to be obedient I had to remain humble by not taking ownership of my service and that I was to simply be a devoted man. Yet there was a part of me that was struggling with the thought that God might be calling us back to do a ministry relaunch because he was disappointed in me, and that this transition period was some form of his discipline; that this transition was somehow him showing me his displeasure in what I had been doing. Had I missed the opportunity to be used by him because I had been prideful? Because I hadn't learned how to walk in humility soon enough? Was the reason I was being asked to give up everything, come back, and start over again because I had lost the ability to be a man of faith? I wasn't the prodigal son, and yet I wasn't the good son—would the Father still be waiting, watching, and looking for me?

This was my thought pattern as I sat in our little room contemplating all that we had talked about, and yet I realized in a moment that all these thoughts were born of fear. Fear that God's love had reached its limit with me. And it was through these glasses of fear that I was viewing our situation. I had indeed lost sight of God's love, and that is why I was struggling with feeling confident in what God was calling my wife and me to do.

As that realization hit me, God illuminated His love to me by bringing me to His Word, and I felt His guiding as I opened up the Bible to Romans 5 where I read this: "When we were utterly helpless, Christ came at just the right time and died for us sinners. Now, most people would not be willing to die for an upright person, though someone might perhaps be willing to die for a person who is especially good. But God showed his great love for us by sending Christ to die for us while we were still sinners. And since we have been made right in God's sight by the blood of Christ, he will certainly save us from God's condemnation. For since our friendship with God was restored by the death of his Son while we were still his enemies, we will certainly be saved through the life of his Son."

If God had loved me when I was a complete enemy and completely opposed to Him, why would He stop loving me now that I was trying to live for Him? Why was I so afraid of His displeasure?

It was then that God brought the passage in Romans 8 to my mind, "And I am convinced that nothing can ever separate us from God's love. Neither death nor life, neither angels nor demons, neither our fears for today nor our worries about tomorrow—not even the powers of hell can separate us from God's love. No power in the sky above or in the earth below—indeed, nothing in all creation will ever be able to separate us from the love of God that is revealed in Christ Jesus our Lord."

With tears rolling down my cheeks, I bowed my head in my little bedroom and prayed, "Lord, forgive me for doubting your love and thinking that your love had a limit when applied to me. Help me, Lord, to trust you, fill me up with an understanding of your love. Let it become a reality in my life, and help me to hear you!"

As soon as I opened my eyes, I felt a confidence that had been missing for quite some time. There was a confidence in our decision of coming back for the ministry relaunch that had not been there before. There was a deep feeling of satisfaction and wholeness knowing that I was not alone, that God was not angry with me, and that I was loved. I had a strong confidence in knowing that God was hearing my prayers and an assurance that I was hearing Him!

Chapter 7 Verses to Consider:

"And we are confident that he hears us whenever we ask for anything that pleases him. And since we know he hears us when we make our requests, we also know that he will give us what we ask for."

1 John 5:14–15 (NLT)

"When we were utterly helpless, Christ came at just the right time and died for us sinners. Now, most people would not be willing to die for an upright person, though someone might perhaps be willing to die for a person who is especially good. But God showed his great love for us by sending Christ to die for us while we were still sinners."

Romans 5:6–8 (NLT)

"Whatever is good and perfect is a gift coming down to us from God our Father, who created all the lights in the heavens. He never changes or casts a shifting shadow."

James 1:17

"Such love has no fear, because perfect love expels all fear. If we are afraid, it is for fear of punishment, and this shows that we have not fully experienced his perfect love."

1 John 4:18 (NLT)

CHAPTER 8

OUR WORTH

"What gives people worth, Mike?" Hal asked one day as he and I were sitting in our usual spot outside the coffee shop enjoying our hot Guatemalan-blend coffees. We had been talking about several different things when the topic of our conversation suddenly turned to the subject of worth.

I thought for a moment about a reply, but I had known Hal long enough now to realize he was heading somewhere, so instead I asked, "Could you explain that? What do you mean?"

Hal leaned back in his chair with a smile and crossed his legs before continuing, "I mean how do people evaluate one's worth to society?" This question caused me to pause and reevaluate where this conversation was heading. *Interesting*, I thought, *he always seems to address the area I am struggling with most.* This question had hit a bullseye!

Hal continued without waiting for a response, "of the saddest things in the world is how people judge others' worth based on their money and possessions! But what's even sadder is how people base their self-worth on these same things. I think, Mike, if you are honest you have done the same to yourself." My eyes had been glued to the table during this statement. I could feel my chest starting to tighten as my breathing was getting heavier. I knew where he was headed and I didn't like it!

Earlier in the conversation, I had been talking with Hal about my financial struggles and the fact that I had seen about 80 percent of our committed support stop due to external circumstances. As a missionary this can happen from time to time, but what I found extremely difficult was raising new support. I mean it seemed like everyone saw the need in Japan for more missionaries and churches, but when it came to making a decision about joining with us financially, the vast majority of people simply declined with the set phrase—"You guys are doing a good job! We will be praying for you guys!" And that would usually be the last we would ever hear from them. This had begun to take its toll on me, as I had started to feel like maybe my ministry wasn't worth supporting, assuming people didn't have confidence in me or in what was being done.

What made this even more difficult was that we were still supporting the ministry in Japan, so all of our available funds that we were getting was going to cover expenses there, which left my family of seven barely anything to survive on in the States. To make matters worse, I had to take my wife up to the USCIS (United States Customs and Immigration Services) Office in Montgomery for a mandatory interview, and I had no money to fix a warped tire that needed to be changed and to get the necessary gas to get there and back.

Hal had in the course of the conversation asked about our financial state, and I had expressed to him our struggles and the need I had. He had surprised me by asking how much we needed for the fix and the gas, and I had hemmed and hawed to answer as I found asking for money directly to be extremely sensitive and uncomfortable. I had managed to change the topic of conversation, but now through a strange turn of events, Hal had brought the conversation around to this subject.

"Well, that's easier to say when you have lived a successful life and don't have to worry about money anymore," was my quiet reply.

I knew the proper response to this question would have been agreement, but there was a part of me that felt this way to a certain extent. As my wife and I continued to see a loss of our committed support, it was causing us to struggle with our feelings of self-worth not just as missionaries but also as believers and people. We had even had conversations that ran like this, "If I'm not a missionary, what use am I? What if no one supports us and we lose everything—other missionaries went to universities where they got practical degrees, my degree is in Biblical Studies, with a pastoral major and biblical language minor—what good is that in the secular world? I am thirty-six years old; it's too late to start over, and yet I am of no value to society or my family if I can't even provide a house and the basics.

Hal looked at me kindly and addressed my soul with these words, "Mike, **your value doesn't come from things; what you can do or what you have. Because God loves you, there is not enough money in the world to represent your worth to Him!**"

His words had struck my cracked and weary heart like the first rain on a drought-stricken field. It was simultaneously painful and refreshing. It was painful because it sounded too good to be true, and yet I yearned for that to be true! My whole life I had been raised hearing the Bible verse that a man who cannot provide for his own family was worse than an infidel, and yet I was following a path in my life that had no great opportunities for wealth, possessions, or advancement opportunities. I had dedicated myself to the ministry, so therefore I had had to find my worth in my doing, and yet Hal had just said that is not what God was looking at! It is not how he evaluated me.

I found that thought extremely refreshing! That God would find value in me even as I struggled to find value in myself was a thought that I wanted to accept, and yet there was still something I couldn't shake.

Hal seemed to sense this because he pressed in on the money issue that I had hemmed and hawed on from earlier. "Mike, why do you find it so hard to talk to people about money?"

The idea of separating my worth from a dollar amount was so foreign to me; I mean we literally identify people by their net worth. If I were honest, this was why I struggled to talk to people about money, because I felt like I was asking them to give of their worth and contribute to mine and hopefully not do it out of pity. I could ask people to give to the ministry because the ministry was worth it, but when it came to specific needs and specific dollar amounts my family or I needed, I felt uncomfortable in sharing them directly one on one with people. Not because my family wasn't worth it, but because my need showed that I was that man whose worth was equivalent to scum. Truthfully, there was a shame I felt in my lack.

"I can't help how I feel," was my lazy, lackluster reply.

Hal wasn't having any of it. "You're talking out of pride."

This statement pierced my thoughts like an arrow to the heart. It was pride! I was prideful in determining my own worth and that wasn't from God, and suddenly I remembered the verse in 1 Corinthians where it says, "You are not your own, you have been bought with a PRICE." As I thought on this, a sudden thought shook me to my core as I realized the PRICE had been God himself and there is no way a price tag could ever be laid on God or his sacrifice that he made for me. If God was willing to pay such a high price for me, why was I demeaning myself by associating my worth with a dollar amount or the contributions I make to society?

Hal wasn't done, though. He had one more word of wisdom for me: "Mike, if we allow the dollar to define our worth, who are we truly serving? Remember because HE loves you there is not enough money in the world to represent your worth!"

This last statement completely broke through to me! It was like a lightbulb had been flipped on in my heart, and as the light came, I felt the chains of pride, negative self-image, and the burden of the world's system of thought break. I felt free and I suddenly no longer felt bound to my shame.

God did indeed provide for our financial needs; for both the tire and gas, and we were able to make it to Montgomery for the interview. And for the first time, I had felt no shame in asking for needed help. I was no longer bound!

This was all too much to comprehend, and yet later that evening as I lay in my bed thinking again over my conversation with Hal, I remembered Jesus' words in Matt. 6 where he says, "Look at the birds. They don't plant or harvest or store food in barns, for your heavenly Father feeds them. And aren't you far more valuable to him than they are?... And if God cares so wonderfully for wildflowers that are here today and thrown into the fire tomorrow, he will certainly care for you. Why do you have so little faith?" Matthew 6:26, 30 (NLT)

As I thought on these verses, I suddenly remembered one more in Psalm 139 where the psalmist writes in verses 17-18, "How precious are your thoughts about me, O God. They cannot be numbered! I can't even count them; they outnumber the grains of sand! And when I wake up, you are still with me!"

These verses were suddenly coming vividly to life, and in the weight of these revelations I started to cry as I realized that God valued ME, that I was precious to Him, and that He finds enough worth in me to love me even though I had felt unlovable. In the midst of contemplating the sheer weight and magnitude of this revelation, a fresh thought hit me as I lay there crying on my bed: *BE STILL and know that I am God.*

This had been God's charge through the Psalmist to the people of Israel. God did not command the Israelites to go out defeat everyone and proclaim him great; instead, God commanded them to be still, and God himself would make himself great! Their job, my job, was to be still—to find my worth and value and purpose in just BEING with him. Not in the having or the doing, but in the being! And that is when it struck me that the favor of God is worth more than all the money this world had to offer, and in God there is no lack of any good thing.

As I lay there marveling at this beautiful revelation of God's love toward me, I was humbled, and I began thanking God. As I did, joy came overflowing to me. I might not own a lot or have a lot of money or talents, but I am of great value to God, and I can be content in knowing that I am His.

Chapter 8 Verses to Consider:

"Don't you realize that your body is the temple of the Holy Spirit, who lives in you and was given to you by God? You do not belong to yourself, for God bought you with a high price. So you must honor God with your body."

1 Corinthians 6:19–20 (NLT)

"Look at the birds. They don't plant or harvest or store food in barns, for your heavenly Father feeds them. And aren't you far more valuable to him than they are? Can all your worries add a single moment to your life? And why worry about your clothing? Look at the lilies of the field and how they grow. They don't work or make their clothing, yet Solomon in all his glory was not dressed as beautifully as they are. And if God cares so wonderfully for wildflowers that are here today and thrown into the fire tomorrow, he will certainly care for you. Why do you have so little faith?"

Matthew 6:26–30 (NLT)

"What is the price of five sparrows—two copper coins? Yet God does not forget a single one of them. And the very hairs on your head are all numbered. So don't be afraid; you are more valuable to God than a whole flock of sparrows."

Luke 12:6–7 (NLT)

"How precious are your thoughts about me, O God. They cannot be numbered! I can't even count them; they outnumber the grains of sand! And when I wake up, you are still with me!"

Psalms 139:17–18 (NLT)

CHAPTER 9

Unconditionally Unconditional

"Welcome to my alma mater!" I jokingly exclaimed to Hal as I met him in the visitor parking lot of the campus of my former college days. We had decided to break from the norm and try a different coffee shop just to spice things up a little. It just so happened that the next closest coffee shop to our usual place was the newish coffee shop on the campus of my alma mater.

The coffee shop was surprisingly comfortable and carried a very strong college vibe. It felt like a mixture of fresh hopes and dreams and homework all mixed together with a smattering of new potential "marriage material" relationships.

Hal and I ordered our coffees and went to sit down in some of the comfy sofa chairs scattered around the shop. We spent a few minutes catching up, and then Hal asked how I was doing. My response was almost animated. "I'm fine. I'm doing great! How are you?"

Hal looked at me for a minute. "Are you really doing great?"

I tried my best to smile and put on a brave face. I didn't want every get-together to be about me and my problems.

"Yeah—things are great!" was my reply, but the truth was everything was far from great! The more that my wife and I were looking at coming back to the States for a ministry relaunch, the more things kept getting unsure, frightening, and stressful. But that was my problem, and I was not going to burden Hal with it!

Hal seemed to accept my response, and the conversation moved on to our recent projects and ideas. The longer we continued to talk, I noticed Hal would look at me strangely for a moment and then continue. Finally he looked at me directly and said, "Mike, you seem to have a hefty burden weighing on you, and it is coming through you as we are talking. What is going on? What are you struggling with?"

I truthfully have never met a man more gifted with discernment than Hal, and I knew that it would be pointless trying to keep anything from him, so I opened up the bag and unloaded all my fears, worries, and cares on him. I explained all about the uncertainty and fear that we were experiencing with following God's call to come back to the States. I honestly didn't care if he was going to judge me, I was just happy to finally express out loud everything that was pent up inside.

Hal listened respectfully, but as I paused to take a breath, he interjected a question: "Mike, why are you so fearful and uncertain? I know you have given me external reasons like money, housing, vehicles, and a lack of clarity in the future of your ministry, but you haven't explained why. So why?"

This gave me pause for a moment as I chewed on this question, but it didn't take long! I knew where this fear was coming from.

"Hal, I feel like a loser! I feel like God is not very pleased with me right now! I mean I haven't done anything he could look at and say, 'Well done, good and faithful servant' to in quite some time. I feel like God is perhaps a little irritated with me. And I feel like the Children of Israel in the wilderness who are always asking incessantly for things and yet are still disobedient and rebellious and complainers! I feel like God is simply putting up with me and is constantly saying, 'Pull yourself together! Stop being a baby! There are more important things at play in the world than you and your problems!' I have all these fears, Hal, and the worst one is I feel like a burden to God!"

Hal looked at me with concern in his eyes. "Mike, I think you're still struggling with the love of God!"

When he said this, I went back in my head to our previous conversations. I felt I had understood and accepted the topics of God's love in regards to hearing Him and with regard to the topic of worth. I had accepted these truths, so what was Hal saying? What did my fear and uncertainty about the future have to do with struggling with God's love? Even as I was thinking this, Hal continued with a truth that stopped my runaway thoughts cold.

"God's love is unconditional, Mike! So stop trying to put conditions on it! It is unquantifiable so stop trying to quantify it!"

It was like a glass of cold water in my face, and I was suddenly wide-awake! I realized that I had indeed been putting conditions on God's love, and this was the reason why I had been struggling so much with fear and stress. The realization of this thought was appalling to me! And even as I recognized the truth of that statement, I felt like once again God must be facepalming himself while shaking his head at Mike the Moron!

Hal wasn't done, though: "Mike, what if I told you that you were in the top tier of those that God loves? Would you believe that?"

I wasn't sure how to answer this question, and truthfully it made me feel uncomfortable. "Umm, compared to whom? Unsaved people, dead people, other Christians? What are the criteria that qualify me to the rank of top-tier love?" I questioned.

"You're missing the point. I asked do you believe that you are in the top tier of those that God loves."

"Compared to whom?!" came my instantaneously irritated response!

Hal looked at me calmly, kindly, and gave me a few minutes to collect myself. Seeing that I had indeed managed to do so, he continued. "I asked if you believed it. I didn't say compared to anyone—there are no comparisons in the body of Christ, Mike! Many people struggle to realize just how much God loves them as an individual. The sacrifice of the

Messiah was with you and me in all of our entirety specifically, individually in mind! He loves you that much and there is nothing you can say or do that will change that!

This truth hit me like a ton of bricks. I had never thought that way before, and to even begin to truly believe that the Messiah's sacrifice was made with me in all of who I was, who I wasn't, and who I pretended to be was mind-blowing! It almost felt like it was too much love! It was overwhelming!

And yet I would continue to struggle with believing it for several days because of my negative self-image, and my own twisted logic of thinking that I had the right to determine just how much God could love me and how much of me he accepted.

As a result, several days later I was still struggling with fear, stress, and a bit of depression. Finally it was getting too much, so I grabbed my sandals and headed for the door. "I'm going for a walk!" I called out to my wife as I made my way out the door.

It was a uniquely beautiful evening that reminded me so strongly of the music video "Vanilla Twilight" by Owl City. The temperature was absolutely perfect but my emotions were bubbling over, and as I got to the base of the driveway I started a furious one-way argument with God. I was letting it all out—I was confessing everything to God, asking for his forgiveness, and pleading with Him for help! I needed to know that He had not abandoned me, and that is when I started asking for a greater revelation of His love!

By this point I was about six blocks into a one-mile circuit, and I was rounding a corner that would bring me to another four-block stretch. As I rounded the corner praying this aloud, I was suddenly brought up short by the most amazing sight in front of me. For directly in front of me just above the rooflines was the largest most vibrant rainbow I had ever seen! Each color was distinct, and the width of the rainbow was easily as wide as the houses it was above! And it was there in that moment of being confronted with such incredible beauty that I heard a small tiny voice in my head.

It said, ***My promise still stands.***

In an instant all my fear, stress, and depression were gone as I considered the weight of this declaration. The rainbow had been a promise to Noah and his descendants that God would never again flood the entire earth. The rainbow was a visible testament of God's promises, and yet it had been years since I had last seen even a decent resemblance to a rainbow—what about these early descendants of Noah? This thought caused me to pause as I considered the ramifications. I am sure that those who left the ark told stories to their children and their children's children. I am sure there might have been a level of worry every time it started to rain, and I wondered if they ever worried that the rainbow might no longer be around as it is not always visible. Did they question the promises and love of God too?

But on this day hundreds and thousands of years after Noah, God's promise was still standing even though the inhabitants of earth hadn't embraced the Lord and instead had filled the earth with violence, anger, immorality, and every imaginable kind of wickedness. They did not deserve the promise God gave to Noah and his descendants! Yet His promise still stands!

WOW! My only possible response to this truth was awe as I thought, *Truly, how great is his faithfulness!* Even as I was chewing on that, I realized the promise of Jesus—when he said he would never leave us nor forsake us. And later in scripture when Paul is trying to describe the love of Christ, he says it is completely unimaginable in its depth and width!

As I walked for four blocks bathed in the magnificence of His faithfulness to His promises, my heart was overwhelmed with the realization that His promise of love to me, Mike Wogsland, still stood. I knew this rainbow was a special gift to me from God. Through it, God showed me that His love was unconditional, unquantifiable, and wholly undeserved, and would stand the test of time and in that knowledge, I felt safe and content in the arms of Christ in a way that I had never known before.

Chapter 9 Verses to Consider:

"This is how much God loved the world: He gave his Son, his one and only Son. And this is why: so that no one need be destroyed; by believing in him, anyone can have a whole and lasting life. God didn't go to all the trouble of sending his Son merely to point an accusing finger, telling the world how bad it was. He came to help, to put the world right again. Anyone who trusts in him is acquitted; anyone who refuses to trust him has long since been under the death sentence without knowing it. And why? Because of that person's failure to believe in the one-of-a-kind Son of God when introduced to him."

JOHN 3:16–18 (MSG)

"For God so loved the world, that he gave his only Son, that whoever believes in him should not perish but have eternal life. For God did not send his Son into the world to condemn the world, but in order that the world might be saved through him."

JOHN 3:16–17 (ESV)

"No, in all these things we are more than conquerors through him who loved us. For I am sure that neither death nor life, nor angels nor rulers, nor things present nor things to come, nor powers, nor height nor depth, nor anything else in all creation, will be able to separate us from the love of God in Christ Jesus our Lord."

ROMANS 8:37–39 (ESV)

"God showed how much he loved us by sending his one and only Son into the world so that we might have eternal life through him. This is real love—not that we loved God, but that he loved us and sent his Son as a sacrifice to take away our sins."

1 JOHN 4:9–10 (NLT)

"The Lord your God is in your midst, a mighty one who will save; he will rejoice over you with gladness; he will quiet you by his love; he will exult over you with loud singing."

Zephaniah 3:17 (ESV)

CHAPTER 10

True Honor

With a loud groan, I rolled over and looked at my phone. The digital face on my iPhone flashed to life and displayed the time—8:20. *What!?* 8:20! I had a meeting scheduled with Hal for 8:30. *Oh, man!* I thought to myself, *I am so late!* I was going to be late for a meeting with Hal at our usual coffee shop. For some reason, I had just had the hardest time trying to wake up and focus, and now as I hurriedly washed the sleep out of my eyes and frantically combed my messy hair to one side, I was going to be a few minutes late for this meeting. Now to some people this might not seem like a bad thing, but to me being late was one of the greatest no-nos in my book. I grabbed the keys, jumped in the car, and quickly made my way to the coffee shop. I could see that Hal was already sitting in our spot with our coffees ordered, and so with a sinking feeling I got out of the car and made my way over to the table bowing my head in a very Japanese fashion and offering my most humble apologies for being late. Hal just smiled. "It's quite all right," he said, "I was able to get the coffees so that we would be ready to talk."

I was so embarrassed! I usually never ran late, and if I did, it was usually because of a major emergency. The level of embarrassment I felt was distracting my thoughts as I contemplated how annoyed he must be with me, and that I was with myself.

Hal could see that I was in a unique mood, so he asked me why.

Looking at him, I explained that as I had been living in Japan for the last ten years, I had picked up on some of their unique tendencies. Being late in Japan was a huge no-no. In fact, in some cases if you were 15 minutes early for a meeting or for work, you were already late. It was considered extremely dishonorable to be late, as it conveyed a real lack of respect and honor for the other person that you were meeting.

Hal laughed. "Well, it's quite different here in America," came his jovial reply. "Americans have a different timetable than Japanese people. So you're quite all right in my book."

I nervously laughed and thanked him, and to be safe I apologized again for being late one last time.

Hal laughed. "Let's talk about honor and shame, Mike. You often talk about Japan as an honor/shame culture, so let me ask you: what do you mean when you say *honor*, and what does honor mean to you?

I opened my mouth to reply, and as I did, I had the sudden realization that my mind was as blank as a mountain covered in fresh powdered snow. I had nothing!

What in the world?!

This was my topic—I talked about honor/shame cultures all the time, and yet here I was struggling to define honor. *It's too early*, I thought to myself, *and I also haven't had any coffee yet.* That might be the problem! So I reached down and picked up the warm, enticing cup of coffee and took a nice long drink of freshly brewed Brazilian goodness, all the while somehow hoping that this magical elixir would give me the answers I was looking for. Unfortunately, it wasn't working fast enough. So eventually, because I didn't want it getting odd that I was drinking for so long, I set the cup of coffee down. Slowly I started to describe everything that honor was not, hoping against hope that maybe Hal would fill in the blanks for himself and be able to define honor through the process of elimination.

Hal wasn't biting, though. And he pressed me to find an answer.

True Honor

Great, I thought; first I am late, and now I am getting embarrassed because I can't answer a question that I should know!

After several more minutes of silent struggles, I was finally able to describe honor as deep respect.

"Is that how you would describe it in Japan?" came Hal's reply.

After a few more moments of thought, I started to formulate an answer that I knew was true. Honor was a way of paying great esteem to someone who deserved it because of their position, worth, or lifestyle/character. I explained, "In Japan, the talk of honor was the driving factor of previous generations, but nowadays honor is not as important as the ability to not bring shame upon one's name, family, business, or cultural group. In fact, many people in Japan are told not to bring shame upon their family or to not be the shame in their family."

Hal folded his hands and put them under his chin. For a few moments he was silent as he gazed with an intense look on his face at the table before finally lifting his head to reply.

"What about you, Mike—if you're honest, isn't this what you've been doing with your ministry?"

I was taken back by this question. I could tell that Hal was not trying to be mean or critical of me or the ministry in Japan, and yet at the same time I found the question profoundly painful! "What do you mean by that?" I asked, more than a little defensively.

"Every time we talk about your ministry in Japan, I can clearly see you love the Japanese people and Kyoto, but almost immediately you start trying to justify your ministry there by what you have done. It seems as if you are trying to avoid shame of some kind."

Deep down in the deepest parts of my soul I knew he was speaking the truth, but I was trapped! *To acknowledge it would bring even more shame*, I thought to myself. And it was then that Hal would give me a spiritual truth that would so wreck my ego and yet build me up all at the same time.

"Honor is important! And God will not share his honor with you, Mike; it is not yours to take!"

It was as if a tidal wave had just crashed over me and I was pinned under the weight of what he had just said. I had never thought in this way before. The longer I considered what Hal had said, the more I realized the truth of what he was saying. There was a difference between honor and not being a shame. Not being a shame did not mean being honorable. As I started to comprehend this, I was able to see that I had indeed been trying to heap up enough good deeds to cover or make up for some preconceived lack of physical success in my church, my ministry, and even my life.

Had I done good things? Yes, but as I thought on it more, it wasn't because I was that good, but rather because God had been that good—I could not take any credit for any of the successes in my life or the ministry, because I had not been the one who brought them about. As soon as that thought crossed my mind, I realized that I had indeed been trying to take the credit away from where the credit was due. I had been trying to steal God's honor in order to make myself seem more important, influential, and successful.

With a shudder that must have been visible, I turned my attention back to the conversation at hand.

Hal noticed my bodily response, though, and kindly called for my attention one more time, "Mike, **God will not share his honor with you, but he honors you by having called you as one of his sons!** Mike, when you are sharing the good news with people, you are not reaching up for people's attention from a position of inferiority, you are reaching down from a declared position of honor as a son of God!"

This last statement had stunned me—I felt disoriented, and the rest of our meeting seemed to pass by in a blur. The disorientation didn't start to dissipate until we got up from our chairs to say goodbye.

With a wave, I grabbed his now empty coffee cup along with mine and made my way inside to throw them away. As I did, I couldn't escape the truth of his words! I barely managed to make it to the fifteen-passenger van we were borrowing before the floodgates opened, and I found myself bawling in the front seat. I didn't care what any of the passersby might be thinking—I was wrecked inside!

Ever since I had been little, I had felt like a drain on people—I was the sick kid who, because of brain cancer, would spend hours of his early life in various hospitals and, as a result, I always felt like I was hindering my family financially. When I could go to school, I felt like I was a hindrance in the classrooms because I was the weird kid everyone had to be careful around because they thought I was sick and fragile and might die if sneezed on. I felt like I was a drain on the teachers as they and everyone seemed to know that teaching me was a waste of time. I was going to have another episode with spinal meningitis or something else, and I was gonna get reset to a point where I'd have to learn how to walk and talk again.

I always felt there was a huge lack in me that I had to make up for, and I realized that I had been trying to steal God's honor for a long time as I was trying to no longer be the shame of my reality. And yet Hal had said that God honors me by calling me as one of his sons—not a casual friend, sometime acquaintance, or troublesome bother! I had not been approaching people as a son of God, but rather as a stranger who would try to prove himself in order to hopefully have the opportunity to share a good story with someone. Because, let's be honest, anything in and of myself was a good story, but it was not good news—good news came from a place of security in knowing who I was and whose I was.

I found it easier to identify as a slave for Christ, but I felt like a drain being a son. I knew this was not the proper mindset for a believer, let alone a pastor and missionary, but this is where I was, and I noticed that I had been living subconsciously in this mindset for a long time and it had been affecting every area of my life! It was like I had been covering the symptoms for years, but now I was confronted with the reality of this cancerous thought!

It was then that I remembered the story of Jesus and the rich man. In the story, the man asks Jesus which commands he should keep for eternal life. Jesus gives him a few, and the rich man replies that he has kept all of them. Jesus then challenges him with one more thing—to sell everything and follow him. As I was thinking about this verse, I realized I had always taken this to mean he loved money more than God, but on this day I saw something different. It wasn't money he loved more than God, it was a question of where his confidence was. This man's confidence was in his wealth; my confidence had been in my own efforts of trying to avoid being a drain and burden, and even in my own efforts to not be the shame of my existence! I realized that so long as my confidence was based in anything other than his love, I didn't truly understand what it meant to be a son of God and what is meant when the Bible talked about God as my father!

With tears pouring down my face sitting in that van, I looked to the sky and gave over all my insecurities to God! I rejected my own efforts of trying to accrue an honor that was not given from Him. And I asked God to forgive me for having confidence in my own efforts apart from His love! As I prayed, I started feeling a calm assurance of God's love that was producing a desire in me for knowing Him more as my father and being content in only what He had to say about me! In that car, God birthed a desire in me to be still and content in the confidence and reality that I am an honored son.

Chapter 10 Verses to Consider:

"In the year that King Uzziah died I saw the Lord sitting upon a throne, high and lifted up; and the train of his robe filled the temple. Above him stood the seraphim. Each had six wings: with two he covered his face, and with two he covered his feet, and with two he flew. And one called to another and said: 'Holy, holy, holy is the Lord of hosts; the whole earth is full of his glory!'"

Isaiah 6:1–3 (ESV)

"There is none holy like the Lord: for there is none besides you; there is no rock like our God."

1 Samuel 2:2 (ESV)

"And they sing the song of Moses, the servant of God, and the song of the Lamb, saying, "Great and amazing are your deeds, O Lord God the Almighty! Just and true are your ways, O King of the nations! Who will not fear, O Lord, and glorify your name? For you alone are holy. All nations will come and worship you, for your righteous acts have been revealed."

Revelation 15:3–4 (ESV)

"For God is the King of all the earth; sing praises with a psalm! God reigns over the nations; God sits on his holy throne."

Psalms 47:7–8 (ESV)

"Therefore God has highly exalted him and bestowed on him the name that is above every name, so that at the name of Jesus every knee should bow, in heaven and on earth and under the earth, and every tongue confess that Jesus Christ is Lord, to the glory of God the Father."

Philippians 2:9–11 (ESV)

"And what union can there be between God's temple and idols? For we are the temple of the living God. As God said: 'I will live in them and walk among them. I will be their God, and they will be my people. Therefore, come out from among unbelievers, and separate yourselves from them, says the Lord. Don't touch their filthy things, and I will welcome you. And I will be your Father, and you will be my sons and daughters, says the Lord Almighty.'"

2 Corinthians 6:16–18 (NLT)

"So you have not received a spirit that makes you fearful slaves. Instead, you received God's Spirit when he adopted you as his own children. Now we call him, 'Abba, Father.' For his Spirit joins with our spirit to affirm that we are God's children. And since we are his children, we are his heirs. In fact, together with Christ we are heirs of God's glory. But if we are to share his glory, we must also share his suffering."

Romans 8:15–17 (NLT)

CHAPTER 11

The Will of the Father

As I come to the last chapter, I am given pause as I thought back to my conversations with Hal. In just a short time this man had gone from being a complete stranger to a true friend. And as I reflected on how he had been teaching me how to translate and understand the love of God in my life and experiences, I realized that there was another conversation that had been woven through our relationship from the very first conversation through to the last.

It was coming to grips with and fully giving into the sovereignty of God. Now before you tune me out and close this book, give me a few more minutes of your time as I explore for you the thread of conversation that completely embraced all of our meetups. It illuminated my eyes to a glorious truth that has not only increased my confidence in the Lord and his plans but also given me the fortitude to stand in times of uncertainty and suffering, all the while simultaneously removing my desire to demand the why. I may not know the answer to the why for you and others, but I know the why for myself. That is what this string of conversations on translating the love of God in my life has shown me!

From our very first meeting, Hal brought up the Sovereignty of God as a reason for giving thanks *for* the troubles, struggles, and trials of this life. At the time I had deflected that portion of the conversation as I didn't want to begin to think that God would ever bring trouble into a believer's life, at the time I believed it was my own mistakes that brought about troubles in my life, because to associate my trouble as God-ordained sounded wrong. Looking back, I have been given the perspective to see that God was expanding my sphere of influence. It's like the words that were said to Corrie Ten Boom from her sister Betsie in the Nazi prisoner camp, "They will listen to you because you have been here!" My struggles, troubles, and trials—all of them—were part of His greater loving plan. Upon seeing that, it made the truth come so much more alive that I need to be thanking God *for* them, because that will allow me to experience a joy not of this world as I go through them!

Hal would again bring up the sovereignty of God in the conversation about obedience and humility. He insisted that our obedience, the ***only*** obedience that would please God, was an *obedience* that was born of him. At the time I struggled with this concept in regards to sovereignty, because I felt that obedience was a choice that I would make and was entirely dependent on me and the efforts I put forth and made. As the conversation flowed into humility, the theme of God's Sovereignty stayed the same, for the vital principle in remaining humble is never taking ownership. As I explored through this at length with Hal, he would consistently and courageously keep calling for me to consider this question: who was on the throne of my life? Was I trying to occupy the throne by taking ownership of my calling, ministry, and destiny, or was I submitting to God and bowing my very essence to him as He ***is*** truly on the throne?

To some this may seem like a pointless and boring struggle—I mean who is gonna argue with allowing God on the throne? Right!? But as I looked at my life, my family, my dreams, my aspirations, and fears, I struggled fully releasing these to God. Some small part of me thought that if I released it to God, he would take it all away or worse. Realizing that the sovereignty of God was actually playing itself out in love in my life, family, dreams, and aspirations and that God had given me those because he had a purpose and a plan that he wanted to carry out helped me to release my tightly wrapped fingers around my notions of control. It helped me to step off the throne and submit to God knowing that his way is best and that I was simply to follow him, go where he goes, do what he does, and say what he says! In the realization of what was expected of me, I found that humility is the Law and the Love of God imprinted on our hearts that allows us to live in the power of God and provides true freedom!

As we continued to get together, Hal would repeatedly weave the sovereignty of God as we looked into the areas of pride and devotion! As Hal lovingly showed me the truth and error of my pride, the reality of the truth that we cannot accept the blame without secretly wanting the credit and later when he would show me that a devoted man doesn't own his own life was lifechanging! Through it all, Hal continued to show that the sovereignty of God was the driving force of it all.

For to take the credit or blame for anything was to elevate ourselves to a position of self-worship. We honestly cannot take credit for the things we do—there is not a single person who has created himself without the assistance or influence of anyone, and that assistance and influence was God working as the master artisan. He is in the process of creating a jar designed to be filled with His love simply for His good pleasure of then having that love overflow from our jar to others. As we are not self-made, we have no right to say how we are used and for what purpose we were made. To do so would be ludicrous! And some of my greatest healing both physically and spiritually came in realizing that God was working something out in my life and it was my job to be content in His hands, the hands of the master potter. This allowed me to accept the idea of a ministry relaunch even though the idea of leaving Japan was heartbreaking to me. I finally realized the truth that his plans are best, and I will only be satisfied in being used in the way he created for me to be used—I am simply a devoted vessel of his love. He is the only one worthy of all the honor, glory, power, and praise. It is absolute foolishness for me to try to take that recognition from Him or to try to diminish it in any way, for there is coming a day when His promise will come to pass that every knee in heaven and under heaven will bow and proclaim him as Lord of Lords and King of Kings!

Hal helped show me the sovereignty of God as we discussed the topic of being the Messiah. He helped show me how God desired to create a bride for Himself from the very beginning of the world and time. That He has throughout the ages been creating a bride that would be made of every nation, tribe, and tongue to be known as His body, and that was being prepared for Him on a major and minor level. On a major level in seeing that this bride (His church) was made up of all believers from creation up to now, and that His bride was a culmination of the work that He has been doing throughout all the ages. On a minor level in that He is still crafting his bride to perfection through us today in a very personal, loving, individualistic sense by molding us into the image of his son through discipleship. And as he is molding me through discipleship, His goal is to bring me to the place where I am entirely hidden in Him! Where I look, smell, walk, and talk like Him so that the world no longer sees me but sees Him. And in becoming the Messiah, I am being perfected as his bride! This gives hope in the hard times, strength when I feel weak, and courage to face persecution! Nothing will be able to thwart His plans of preparing me as he sovereignly is preparing His bride!

Finally came the conversations on love and worth, and even here Hal insisted that it was all completely covered and infused by the sovereignty of God. For without God's desire to love, I would have no hope! Because of his great love, I can have confidence that he hears me when I cry out to him and that I, in turn, can hear him. I can have this hope because His love is unconditional and unquantifiable. And the only time I struggle with hearing him, my self-image, and self-worth is when I try to quantify and put conditions on God's love and just how far it can reach! Again, to quote Corrie ten Boom, "There is no pit that God's love is not deeper still!"

As Hal brought me to this place of being able to see the greatness of the love of God, he showed me that it was God's sovereign plan from the beginning of time to lavish his love on me, and not just me but all those who believe. This truth was overwhelming and truly amazing! It gave me confidence in the plans of God as he was working it all out through his love, and this gave me the courage to follow him when he speaks.

Hal insisted that the sovereignty of God was the base of everything; in the beginning I could not understand why he insisted so much on bringing up the topic consistently. That was until I started looking back over our conversations and putting it into the context of my life. That is when things started to come together for me as I saw the plans of God weaving my life into his story. I know my story is not yet finished, and I have confidence that God will make it something beautiful that will bring Him glory. In realizing that, I can look expectantly and hopefully to the day when I stand before God and hear that which my heart yearns for most—"Well done, my good and faithful servant!"

I believe I shall hear this, for I believe that the sovereignty of God and His love will allow me to stand with humble confidence in that day—knowing that it was His will and love working both in me and through me all along! I am so thankful for the friendship and the conversations that I have had with Hal so far, and I look forward to many more to follow! This man helped show me, and clarify for me, several major truths in God's Word that I had been struggling with for so long. While I cannot say that I have achieved perfection by any stretch of the imagination, I can say that I can indeed see the race track clearer and I feel better equipped for the race! I can see now both how to translate and understand the love of God in the season and trials of my life, and in turn I can help express and share that love with others as his disciple. And that is why I wrote this book: to encourage you and hopefully clarify for you the track a little bit more, so that you too can run with confidence for the prize that is set out before you! So that you too can learn how to translate and understand the love of God in your life, and that you will, in turn, be able to help communicate and teach others how they too can understand and communicate the love of God to others because that is the essence of discipleship. Blessings, my friends!

Chapter 11 Verses to Consider:

"Our God is in the heavens, and he does as he wishes."

Psalms 115:3 (NLT)

"Whatever the Lord pleases, he does, in heaven and on earth, in the seas and all deeps."

Psalms 135:6 (ESV)

"At the end of the days I, Nebuchadnezzar, lifted my eyes to heaven, and my reason returned to me, and I blessed the Most High, and praised and honored him who lives forever, for his dominion is an everlasting dominion, and his kingdom endures from generation to generation; all the inhabitants of the earth are accounted as nothing, and he does according to his will among the host of heaven and among the inhabitants of the earth; and none can stay his hand or say to him, What have you done?'"

Daniel 4:34–35 (ESV)

"And we know that for those who love God all things work together for good, for those who are called according to his purpose. For those whom he foreknew he also predestined to be conformed to the image of his Son, in order that he might be the firstborn among many brothers. And those whom he predestined he also called, and those whom he called he also justified, and those whom he justified he also glorified."

Romans 8:28–30 (ESV)

CHAPTER 12

WHAT ABOUT YOU?

Thankfulness *for* all things is the doorway to unlocking freedom and joy.

SELF EXAMINATION #1: What's going on in your life that is really bad, sad, or mysterious that you could be thankful for?

Our motto should be "Whatever the messiah says, do it!" Obedience is our expression of love to the Messiah—our goal is obedience in everything (prayer, life, marriage, relationships, etc.)

SELF EXAMINATION #2: Is there something God told you to do that you're not doing yet?

The key to remaining humble is to never take ownership. Humility is vital in allowing us to move without fear in doing whatever the Messiah asks us to do.

SELF EXAMINATION #3: Is it your purpose or his purpose you are trying to live out?

We can't accept the blame without secretly wanting the credit. Pride and reverse pride are dangerous weights and traps. They can immobilize us by convincing us we tried our best, and they cause us to settle for the status quo.

SELF EXAMINATION #4: Are there areas in your life where you can see the traces of pride and reverse pride? Release it to God!

A devoted person doesn't own his own life.

SELF EXAMINATION #5: Have you bowed every area of your life to the Messiah?

The number one key to hearing God is knowing how much you're loved! If you are struggling to hear God, you are probably struggling with accepting the Messiah's love. He loves you more than you can imagine!

SELF EXAMINATION #6: Are you struggling to hear the voice of God? In what area of your life are you not allowing the Messiah's love to penetrate?

We are to be the Messiah. We are to be so hid in Christ that when the world looks at us, they see the messiah smiling back! This isn't impossible! It starts one minute at a time, then five minutes, 10 minutes, 30 minutes, an hour, etc. We do this by carrying the mind of Christ.

SELF EXAMINATION #7: How can you be the Messiah today to your family, in your work, to your friends, neighbors, etc.? Practice makes perfect!

Because he loves us, there is not enough money in the world to represent it!

SELF EXAMINATION #8: Take a moment or many and contemplate the worth God has in you!

Stop associating your worth to God and this world through the lenses of your accomplishments, financial savings, or titles. Allow God to identify and declare your worth and walk in that confidently!

God's love is unquantifiable and unconditional! Stop trying to quantify or put conditions on it!

SELF EXAMINATION #9: In what ways have you been putting conditions on God's love in your life?

God will not share his honor with us, but he honors us by calling us as his sons and daughters. This comes with security, position, power, and authority both ways—He is the King of all, and we have access to him!

SELF EXAMINATION #10: Contemplate the honor of God and the amount of honor he has paid you! Do you walk in the confidence and mindset of one who is a son or daughter of the King of all Kings? Does this affect how you approach people about the King?

The sovereignty of God in everything allows us to see the whys to the tough questions and situations in our lives.

SELF EXAMINATION #11: Look at and consider the ups and downs, struggles and triumphs of your life. Can you see the picture being painted? Are you able to see the strength you gained, the story that was written, and the voice you have been given for his glory?

Final Thought

We are to be disciples who make disciples. Are you able to see the love of God in and through your life? Are you ready and willing to express what that looks like with someone in some way today?

The key to effective discipleship is time. Hal made himself available to me and allowed me the freedom to argue with him and struggle through these difficult points on my own. Let me challenge you to share with others the freedom that God has given you through his love and make yourself available to others in this process. They may be like me and need some time; there is no need to rush the process, just be there for them!

I believe that opening yourself up and being available for even one person **can** and **will** change the world!

Notes

*All quotes from Corey Ten Boom were acquired from a play based on the book the *Hiding Place*.

Depository, B. (2015). *The Hiding Place: The Triumphant True Story of Corrie Ten Boom: Corrie Ten Boom, John Sherrill, Elizabeth Sherrill: 9780553256697*. [online] Bookdepository.com.

Meet the Man

HAL CALISCH

Hal has been and continues to be a successful businessman, consultant, and life coach. His specialty is in the arena of changing people's lives through discipleship! He does this by consistently and intentionally making time to meet with people and being open to walking life with them. Hal has a burning desire and passion to see people live in the realization and freedom of the love of God. He desires to see the body of Christ lit on fire as they come into this deep, personal, individualized relationship with the Messiah. Hal is collaborating with Mike in the ministry of Translating Love. He resides with his family in Pensacola, Florida.

About the Author

Mike has been privileged to serve the Body of Christ in a variety of different roles—everything from youth pastor to teaching pastor, lead pastor to church planter, pioneer, and missionary. Mike, his wife Seira, and their five children served for over nine years in Japan, with over four years in the center of Kyoto, Japan. They recently returned to the States where Mike is serving as a writer and speaker, and working with Hal Calisch to launch a disciple-making ministry called *Translating Love*. *Translating Love* is dedicated to building disciples on multiple platforms such as conferences, YouTube videos, writing books, and personal relationships. Mike and his family currently reside in Pensacola, Florida.

CPSIA information can be obtained
at www.ICGtesting.com
Printed in the USA
LVOW10s1009030618
579179LV00009B/155/P

9 781595 557728